ReLaunch!

ReLaunch!

SPARK YOUR HEART TO IGNITE YOUR LIFE

HILARY DECESARE

NEW DEGREE PRESS

ReLaunch!
Spark Your Heart To Ignite Your Life

ISBN 979-8-88504-912-2 *Paperback*
979-8-88504-717-3 *Kindle e-book*
979-8-88504-196-6 *E-book*

For my mom, JuJu, for being my constant invisible presence. And to my husband, Erich, for being my visible support and loving me through my ReLaunches.

Photo by Cathy Merenda, Golden Door, September 9, 2019

August 14, 1941–October 28, 2019

FOREWORD

What are the limitations that our parents, teachers, spouses, or bosses put on us? What about our own self-imposed limitations?

Whatever they are and however we got them, the truth is this we have all been conditioned to believe and behave in alignment with our limitations. That's the challenging news. Here's the great news.

We have never seen a better time, or a more critical time, to discover how to take control and to move beyond those limitations. Why not get rid of the things holding you back and change your interpretation of what you believe so you can step into the greatest version of your life?

Yes, it's time for you to ReLaunch!

If you're ready to break free and be happier, healthier, and wealthier to manifest more impact, more contribution, more happiness, more of everything you want, to expand your skills and awareness, Hilary DeCesare's life-changing book is indispensable. It will guide you on how to let go of limitations and start leading with your heart.

Hilary doesn't just teach it; she's lived it herself, and as you follow her story of self-discovery along with expert commentary and inspiring examples, she will illuminate a path to unfold your own powerhouse of possibilities.

—*JOHN ASSARAF, FEATURED IN THE GLOBAL PHENOMENON BOOK AND MOVIE* THE SECRET, *TWO-TIME* NEW YORK TIMES *BESTSELLING AUTHOR, AND LEADING BEHAVIORAL NEUROSCIENCE RESEARCHER*

Intuition

= 3HQ™

PREFACE

When you were a child, did you ever go out on a warm summer night under an inky sky studded with a spangle of stars and a honeydew moon to try to catch fireflies in a jar? Maybe you carried a net and, if you were swift and lucky, managed to trap a few in your jar, little sparks of lightning in a bottle. During challenging times, it seems like everyone is out in the midst of a very long and dark night with their net to find their lightning in a bottle, hoping for some sort of illumination to make sense while facing unparalleled obstacles.

Fortunately, we are all armed. Not with a net and a jar, but with our own internal arsenal—what I call the 3HQ™, the total of our Hearts, Heads, and Higher Selves. The 3HQ™ is the catalyst by which we align our hearts and heads to hear—and listen to—our intuition, leading us to our Higher Selves. When aligned, these elements of our innermost being act as a powerful accelerator in achieving our goals. By creating a process to bring our hidden 3HQ™ to the surface, we can blast through the barriers that stall or even block the transformation to our best selves. The 3HQ™ Method gives us the tools to connect from a place of truth that originates deep inside, an impulse that allows us to find solutions and fulfill our mission in our most aligned and authentic way.

For those of us who grew up in the sixties, seventies, and eighties, it was all about our IQ, the intelligence quotient. Who was smarter? That was the judgment scale. Everything was about cognitive prefrontal cortex, or what is called the thinking brain, where we were taught and where all mysteries and solutions resided.

Then came the monkey wrench in the equation—EQ, the emotional quotient. Research shows that successful leaders have strong emotional intelligence. Emotional intelligence has been defined as understanding one's own emotions and the emotions of others, including the ability to apply emotions to navigate and solve problems. In fact, *this* was the differentiating success factor that set them apart from others with similarly high IQ and skillsets (Bradberry, 2015). It became increasingly evident a symbiotic relationship between our thinking brain and our emotional neurological systems not only exists but is also critical.

No longer can we use just one area of the brain as the measuring stick. Success factors have evolved along with society. Or, rather, the recognition of these factors has evolved. The factors were always there; we are only now widening the window for science and technology to allow us to recognize and understand them. We likely possess multiple intelligences: musical, naturalistic, interpersonal, spatial, and among others, spiritual intelligence, which has been defined as "understanding the sacred, [and] being one" (McGreal, 2013).

For now, the IQ and the EQ are our twin stars—our emotion/heart and our thoughts/head—that set the tone, rotating together as an infinite figure eight, circling within our own personalities. The hidden power of the three Hs—the Heart, Head, and Higher Self—combine to form an innate, values-driven accelerator. When they align as a team, we have the platform to operate as our highest and best version of ourselves. When the barriers to this alignment are removed, the doors open to the path with the outcomes we seek—a relationship, a business, a family—however we individually define self-fulfillment.

Each of us has different goals, but the path to achieve them is similar. As a certified master neuroscience coach, I have developed a formula that lays out a path to transformation of living a lifestyle of 3HQ™, a continuum for a personal trajectory of growth and development powered by the heart and head, while informed by your intuition—those signals that emerge from our deepest selves.

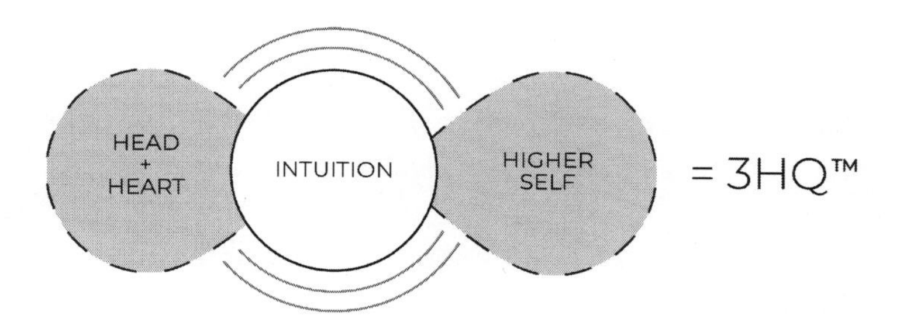

The formula is simple. Achieving it can require work on ourselves since each element lives not only in the present but has tentacles reaching back into our past.

For this reason, the truth of who we are (and why) is often obscured from us, hiding in plain sight as we struggle to understand the basis of our "why"—why things matter, why are we here, why we are making certain choices, and why we want to serve and support others. Linking and aligning these beliefs and actions that originate within our Hearts and our Head with the Higher Self creates this trifecta for ultimate success that shows up as the best version of ourselves, and the transformative rewards that can bring. I believe the key is understanding how to tap into this Higher Self because the Higher Self is the source of your internal energy, connecting to something bigger than you.

We need to understand much of this is beyond the reach of our conscious control. According to the National Science Foundation, 80 to 90 percent of what we believe comes to us pre-programmed from our unconscious mind (Bennett, 2018). Except here's the news: we *do* have control *if* we know how to access it. We can exit the autopilot ramp by locating and surfacing our innermost, deeply buried beliefs—the beliefs that trigger those automatic responses and limit our conscious capabilities. Deconstructing and mastering the calibration of this finely tuned trio, the 3H Quotient, provides an off-ramp from the autopilot rut and puts us in conscious connection and control of our transformation from within. This is the neuro version of looking for those elusive fireflies in the night. But those fireflies—a.k.a. our beliefs and their sparks—are there, and it's up to us to capture them (Oppland, 2021).

Most of us want to be successful, but success is not just about knowing everything and being the smartest brain in the room, or the best at a particular skill. It's about mastering that trifecta: the 3HQ™. This is where the journey to surfacing and mastering those limiting beliefs begins. The key is to learn a success-driven method to master your ability to manifest and deliver on your vision so you can become the force behind making the things you want happen in your life.

The first phase is to acknowledge the most important relationship we can have is with ourselves. We intuitively seek that version of ourselves, the one who shows up as the best possible version—if we listen to our intuition. Have you ever felt a "feeling" in your heart, a "knowing" in your mind, even a "chill" or a "sense" that runs through your body? Your intuition may be speaking. Your heart and your mind are the only way to hear and master your internal, unconscious conversations with yourself *from the inside out* and to go through the process of bringing what is inside of us—for better and worse—to the surface.

The collection of invisible, limiting beliefs and barriers that have been hiding in plain sight can now be brought to the surface, recognized, dealt with, and eradicated. We can give ourselves permission to say, "The old chapter is ending. The next one begins here and now."

Perhaps you are getting a not-too-subtle hint that it's time to begin a relationship with your authentic self, not the one showing up on autopilot. This relationship is the accelerator to taking conscious control and beginning the journey to your ReLaunch. When you ignite the complete 3HQ™ trio of Heart, Head, and Higher Self working in concert, you can access unlimited empowerment of strength, power, and wisdom to take you wherever you define a lifestyle of success and self-love.

Once we awaken our unconscious selves, answers are within our grasp. We are not victims waiting in a tower for "help and rescue." We are fully capable of loving and empowering ourselves, and we can be the victors. With the 3HQ™, we have the engine to reprogram and flip the subconscious beliefs that have psychologically chained us to a life of preconditioned habits. These ingrained beliefs have fused into involuntary habits intended by biology to keep us safe; however, they may also hold us back by setting up seemingly

invisible, immovable guardrails we can't seem to escape (Wiest, 2018; Del Cul, Baillet, and Dehaene, 2007).

Our subconscious brain does not know the difference between hopelessness and an opportunity. As Henry Ford said, "Whether you think you can or think you can't, you are right." Everything is equal in the subconscious. There's no reality, no fantasy, no rationality, no judgment in this head-space! So, if our subconscious embedded habit is to reach for a bag of chips at the danger hour of 2 p.m. every day (yes, I admit, that's me), it has no idea about the calories, cholesterol, and waistline involved. It's up to the conscious—surface—part of our brain to apply the brakes, to say, "I recognize you. You are just a habit. I can change this. That bag of potato chips can stay on the shelf. *Reach for the almonds, Hilary*!" The Potato Chip Principle can apply to many things we'd like to change.

I hope you can see this book as an empowerment manifesto to yourself, not a handbook about "self-help." That is a very limiting and disenfranchising term, in my opinion. Are you primed and ready to remove barriers and speed bumps that stand between yourself and achieving the rewards that purposeful change can bring about in all areas of your life? You are worthy, and you are capable of so much more.

Shout-out to the little girl who chased fireflies and had dreams. It's time to release your fireflies and let them glow in the fresh air of the real you, the woman you have grown up to become. Maybe they've been bottled up in the jar, with the air holes poked through the lid; that was your old self. They've been inside the entire time, knocking on the glass, gasping for air. Now it's time to ReLaunch them and let them fly. With the guidance of this book and the support and sisterhood of our entire collective ReLaunch community, I invite every woman who has a dream to ReLaunch to learn how to activate your 3HQ™, to share how others have achieved their own success, to create that dream, and to take it to the next level ... and *beyond.*

INTRODUCTION

"Hilary, are you sitting down?"

It was August 23rd, 2017, 2:30 p.m. Pacific Standard Time. But I was still on FVT—Family Vacation Time—when my mom called and told me she had thirteen malignant lesions on her liver. She had stage four cancer.

Thirteen. Malignant. Lesions. Three words that changed my world forever, turned everything I thought I knew upside down, made me rethink what I really wanted in my life and how I would make choices and decisions from that minute forward.

I was home in the San Francisco Bay Area, where I had lived for over twenty-five years. Floating on the biggest high, just four days after celebrating a special milestone birthday with thirty of my closest friends and family at Silver Lake, our family's summer cabin, newly rebuilt after a devastating fire. I hadn't even viewed the pictures and videos from my cell phone yet, but certain images were already imprinted on my heart:

Click: My husband, children, dad, stepmom, mom, brother, and best friends were seated at an elegant, white-table-clothed, forty-foot-long table—this new one unworn by decades of kids' messy elbows and passing platters of sweet corn and s'mores. The laughter was infectious as the toasts brought me back to childhood memories, times throughout life I had chosen to forget—yet that night, they made sure I remembered them all.

Click: I had chosen the cabin for my celebration specifically because it had given me an opportunity each year to reflect on my life. I usually made sure to come for my birthday, the halfway point of the year, to set my yearly goals. The cabin had always enveloped me like a loving blanket; the knotty old walls had heard the tears and cheers from marriages, divorces, passings of loved ones, and births of kids. Tragically, a couple of years prior, the eighty-five-year-old cabin had blown up. Thankfully, my dad, stepmom, son, and brother had left it fifteen minutes before it went up in flames and was leveled. We rebuilt the cabin—carefully protecting the resident yellow-spotted endangered frog we didn't even know existed—and two days before my birthday weekend it was ready to usher in the next generation of memories.

Click: Familiar sparkles of silver bouncing off Thunder Mountain, looming powerfully in the distance. If the rebuilt cabin was new, the lake was timeless. The Old Man, as the mountain I had hiked to in my teens had always been called, stood in the horizon off our burnt-out porch, giving out all the wisdom that comes with agelessness. How I wished I could be like that. Strength, power, and wisdom—it seemed to me those core values were all there to be absorbed, like the fragrance of pine in the air, if I could only be evolved enough to let them permeate my inner self.

However, I knew all too well that accessing and changing our thinking is not so simple. Most of our beliefs are buried deep inside our minds, locked in our personal vaults. In my work, I was more than up to the complex challenge of helping clients break through and tap into their innermost selves. I had crafted a consulting business, The ReLaunch Co., to support life transitions—first from liking yourself to loving yourself and your life, then segueing into finding parallel confidence and self-fulfillment in business. I had worked out a science- and fact-based approach, drawing from my research, study, and experience.

Earlier in my career, successful women in Silicon Valley's technology sector were a rarity; I was considered an anomaly, a somewhat unique icon for success, selling Oracle's applications into the big boys' club of some of the world's top businesses. I was often approached for advice, which led me to start my coaching business over twenty years ago. That business was my happy place, and my coaching business had taken off. However, increasingly, my personal life as a mom and my relationships were less aligned.

And so, whenever I was at the cabin, the Old Man of the mountain beckoned me to look inside myself. Then, his job was done. The rest, I knew, was up to me. I knew the steps

involved my heart. I had no problems advising others; however, seeing our own blind spots is never easy. Overcoming my own inertia, the swarming, buzzing thoughts and the distracting tasks at hand—the ones we all seem to have—well, that was another thing altogether.

Click: I focus on my mom, sitting across from me in a canary-yellow lace mini dress, taking the disco-era party theme to another level with her matching yellow go-go boots rising to lead the toasts (only my irrepressible mom could get away with yellow go-go boots). She talked from her heart about love, friendship, the woman I had become, and how proud she was of her girl. It was truly everything I needed and wanted to hear from the person who had been by my side always.

Four days later, I was standing in my Bay Area family room when the familiar caller ID popped up: "JuJu Bean," a.k.a. Judy, my mom. She and I talked at least five times a day, but somehow, that day was different. Her voice was pragmatic and direct, yet distant. "Hilary, they found thirteen lesions in my liver."

What? No. This was my best friend, my confidante, the woman who was supposed to live well into her hundreds, like all the women in my family for four generations. She was only seventy-seven. Three decades had been stolen in those few words. Instead of chatting about the birthday weekend and reveling in the stories of the talent show, silent disco party, and hysterical conversations, we talked about MRIs, prognoses, next steps, and how long she had to live. I had tasted this netherworld myself. Twenty years earlier, I had faced malignant melanoma—in my case, as it fortunately turned out, found and treated in time.

It took me a few seconds to get my bearings as the room swirled around me, feeling like Dorothy in the tornado, but when I landed, I remembered where I was—Medical Oz: The World of the Very, Very Sick. In an instant, not much else mattered. I struggled to remember I had to keep at least some level of a grip for my three teenaged children, yet I knew intuitively things were never going to be the same.

"Mom, what are you saying? Just this weekend you did the seven-mile trail around the lake with thirty of us!" How could this be happening to my mom, who always went to every doctor's appointment for everything she was supposed to? *Thirteen. Malignant. Lesions.* A guttural sound came from somewhere within me as I collapsed into the couch. I was trapped in a deadly Groundhog Day. I knew this place from my stepmom with ovarian cancer, from best friends with breast cancers, from my own encounter with melanoma. It was a very dark space.

My inner neuro coach raised a hand, struggling to be heard: *Hilary, you have to stop these negative thoughts right now!* Of the six thousand thoughts that go through our mind every day, 85 percent are negative—even in the best of times (Antanaityte, 2021). *I said to myself, you've got to pull yourself together if you're going to be of any help to any of us—especially Mom.*

Right! I reflexively snapped into fix-it mode. After decades in Silicon Valley, thriving in the inner circle of technology's Mt. Olympus while working for some of the world's most powerful companies and launching my own entrepreneurial businesses, *fix-it-now* was my default mechanism. Control the situation. Out-think the problem. Run ahead of it, research it, outsmart it, forge the path to the win. Stick with the protocol. Leverage the logic. Hadn't this strategy worked before? Physically, I was in the lucky girl cancer club, and financially, I'd made it into the millionaires' club. Yes! Surely a protocol exists. Surely, this could be handled.

Thirteen. Malignant. Lesions. With those three words, science and rationality hit a roadblock for me. Science and fact—those were my sweet spots to success. Suddenly, my coaching business and my personal life dealing with my mom were colliding. I was not just devastated; I was seriously lost. My head and heart were not just misaligned but in conflict. I realized this would be the most difficult and significant ReLaunch of my life.

But at 1:10 a.m., fourteen months later, I held my mother's hand and saw her take her last breath in a low-lit room as she passed through the transparent veil. My life would never be the same. The timing was right on target. My mom was seventy-eight; in 2019, the median life span for women in the US was 78.9 years (World Bank, 2021). My own belief that I would live into my hundreds was shaken to the core. Many of us, especially women at the mid-zone of life, forty to sixty, have faced similar challenges. Just when we thought we had it nailed, the wheels fall off and we find ourselves spinning, in search of direction.

Does any of this sound familiar? Just when we have become pretty good at being daughters, we wake up one morning and we're the matriarch. Just when we think we've mastered our jobs, the company gets sold. Just when we've become fantastic moms, the kids leave the nest. Just when the empty nest leaves us ripe again for romance, somebody finds it with somebody else. Yikes.

Although shaken by mom's prognosis, I had the hubris to believe my professional training had given me an edge. Neuroscience is fact-driven and, unsurprisingly, I had focused all my energy on the part that can be measured and quantified. Let's break down the numbers: How many courses and certifications could I collect? How many promotions? How many bonuses and shares of founder stock? How many businesses could I launch? How much money was in my bank account, creating my lifestyle?

These things, however, were all on the surface. The rest is buried deep in our subconscious, inaccessible. I was learning firsthand—outside the classroom, the podium, or podcast—that it is very difficult to pull yourself out of a quicksand mindset from *the surface*. You have to dig deep, to the bottom of the pit, to your innermost self, in order to claw your way out. And nobody else can do this for you. The quicksand will always win unless you peel the layers back

like a nesting doll to reveal the inside, the invisible part of you, and listen and tap into your intuition and access your Higher Self—the best possible version of yourself. As I was soon to discover, this transition was the start of the journey. A restart at midlife. After twenty years as an experienced coach and trainer, I had transitioned to the tribe of trainee—like all of us, seeking answers.

Are you aware transitions happen to us all the time? Chances are you have already experienced at least one or two, maybe more. In fact, sociologists who study life transitions estimate most people experience three to five major life transitions—some voluntary and welcome, like falling in love or having a baby, and others unwelcome and challenging, like unemployment, illness, and death. Collective transitions are also a factor—these are shared events such as 9/11, pandemics, and global conflicts—but still, these events are unique for each person (Brooks, 2020). Some make us feel like we can't move forward or might make us feel like we're paralyzed, like we don't have control of anything. Each is unique, yet all are circular, leading us to the next phase of our lives. One phase ends, the next evolves, and a transition begins anew.

But I have come to believe life transitions lead to even more incredible life transformations; everything has a message and is a training ground to get us through from survivor to thriver. I'm convinced a silver lining is in every one of these life transitions. After hosting one hundred twenty-five podcasts on ReLaunches—which included some of the most violent, awful, heart-wrenching situations—I have never had a single person on my show say they would want to go back and change what had happened.

So many insights show that the path to get through all the tough times is by focusing inward; it is the only way to have the outward life we long for after losses and life changes. I've found support from researching, studying, and working with experts like Dr. John Gray of the iconic book *Men Are from Mars and Women Are from Venus*; brain expert John Assaraf, who has been featured in the global phenomenon book and movie *The Secret* and is a two-time *New York Times* best-selling author; neuropsychologist PhD Dr. Shannon Irvine; and Jim Fortin, a world leader in subconscious self-transformation. In this book, I feel fortunate to share with you the amazing stories of women and men who have experienced their own transitions, come out the other side, and found their silver linings by accessing their 3HQ™.

The arc goes like this: transformation to move forward starts on the inside and emanates outward in a ripple effect. Innermost thoughts, repeated often over specific periods of time and with an emotion/feeling attached, can transform to become beliefs.

In turn, beliefs can be either limiting or empowering. They can lead us to take actions that support them. You make the choice: you can either remain stuck—with limiting beliefs holding you back—or break free and clear to create more of the positive beliefs that help you move forward to ignite corresponding actions. Nevertheless, this is an inside job, and you've got to work on the inside to see a difference on the outside (where transformations become visible). This is the process I embarked on when my mother died.

The best teachers have gone through this process themselves—and I was ready to lean in with a new vengeance to shape a positive framework for my personal ReLaunched belief system. I recognized my identity was being restricted by my own old, limiting belief that I had years to live and was only halfway through my life—a neat rationale for postponing decisions or making changes. I realized however long or short, life needed to be lived *now*. What new, authentic identity could possibly be uncovered and created? Not in some misty future, but sooner rather than later? Isn't that what we all want? It was time to force myself to confront and leave my comfort zone, to venture beyond the safe and familiar and be able to share the process so others would not need to wait to start living in abundance and gratitude.

I realized my mission was to serve, help people grow, and inspire women to use the tools to fire up those sparks. You don't need academic degrees. You don't need the business experience, the right relationships, the right pedigree, or the right geography for the optimal life I'm talking about. It's about being open to realizing ReLaunches can be big or small, but all transitions have the potential to lead to ReLaunches that are truly transformational. We must all start the journey to get to the destination.

Today's world has thrown us all into a ReLaunch of some sort—at home, in relationships, and at work. The 2021 "Great Resignation" saw four million Americans quit their jobs

(Cook, 2021). This social tsunami was led by women (Fox, 2021). We are now looking at mass ReLaunches and, as we move into this new age, not a new normal, but a new different.

The question is no longer about the platform of how to "work smarter" and take an IQ test or ace the SAT score. The old equation was based on vertical compartmentalization, IQ and EQ, but today's more relevant platform is based on a striving toward inclusion so we can fire on all cylinders—our Hearts, Heads, and Higher Selves. The increasing mindfulness of the impact of our lifestyle choices is a key driver of this approach. Many of us are simply fed up with the stress and competitiveness that have cut out the heart from the way we have been forced to live for far too long. We are searching for an alignment and sense of purpose that goes beyond the myth of "work/life balance" (Lau, 2020).

No schedule is involved, but upon reaching the midpoint in life, I've noticed one particular convergent theme. When the health and economic environment (over which we have no control) collides with what many of my clients have called a "Mid-Life Crisis" (over which we do have control), there can be a major impact effect.

Grappling with the concept that one's life may be half over thrusts many people into a depressive state in the best of circumstances (Morin, 2021). Yet I see what is happening as an *identity* crisis. This hits people when their expectations of where they should be in life

doesn't map to where they are in either their professional or personal lives, or both. In this case, their self-image is in flux, although this can happen at any point, not just mid-life. In fact, people are constantly re-evaluating—and misunderstanding—their self-identity.

In fact, a 2001 study by Cornell University sociologist Elaine Wethington, the largest study ever done on midlife, found the midlife crisis to be much less common than people believe. According to the study, although more than 25 percent of Americans over age thirty-five think they have had a midlife crisis, more than half of these were actually "stressful life events" (Lang, 2001). Enter the external world and the tsunami that comes with it, and you get an axis of crisis. Heart, Head, and Higher Self—all three elements must work in alignment for balance to be achieved. That's the key to the 3HQ™ Method.

I hope this book, and the 3HQ™ Method as described in its pages, will help you find a pathway to question everything, which is the beginning of finding potential answers and solutions. Why are you doing certain things in a certain way? Why are you prioritizing yourself last? Why do you have the beliefs you do, and are they truly your own? Be aware of your thoughts and the feelings associated with them. Once you've identified that so many of the things you do daily are automatic, you can get to the root of where they originated and cleanse yourself of the holdover beliefs holding you back. Then, you can finally work on rewiring your brain to move forward and achieve whatever lifestyle of success you choose.

As for me, visibly witnessing the awakening of others is when I think I feel Mom's presence the most. I can't see her, but I know she is there with every woman who calls, direct messages, and texts me—because the words speak for themselves about the changes, perceived as magical and crazy, occurring in their lives. Each is the witness to transformational ReLaunches. I hope you feel her irrepressible spirit and my heartfelt support as we celebrate the unique transformational journey of your professional and personal life.

PART ONE

HEART

CHAPTER ONE

PAINTING THE HOUSE

When I was just entering high school, we lived in Bel Air, California, one of the most affluent suburbs in the country—an area where movie stars lived and dogs got pedicures. My parents divorced when I was four years old and both remarried within a year. My stepfather, the president of two banks, came into our lives, and our lifestyle and location shifted. Like most kids, I was focused on myself, school friends, and activities until some big changes happened that I couldn't ignore. Looking back, I now see this was the beginning of a lifelong journey of ReLaunches; at the time, though, I didn't realize the significance.

When I was in my mid-teens my mom, who was passionate about decor and had an eye for detail, decided our big brown house needed to be painted a shade of white to freshen it up. But right around that time, the stock market crash of the eighties suddenly hit. A conglomerate purchased the banks where my stepdad worked, new management came in, and he was let go. To make matters worse, he had personally lost a lot of money in the market. Of course, I didn't realize this, and my mom never even knew the extent of the losses until the money was actually gone. Then things changed almost overnight. If I knew then what I know now, I would have recognized being laid off set my stepdad up for a massive identity crisis. His expectations of where he thought he should be in his life suddenly conflicted and clashed with his "then" reality. Still, I could sense the dynamic of the household had shifted dramatically.

One afternoon, which must have been around the time of the layoff, I overheard a conversation. My mom was talking about having the house painted, and my stepdad said, "Judy, we don't have the money, so we can't paint the house right now."

I was listening from around the corner, and my stomach dropped through the floor. *What? We don't have enough money to paint the house?* All I could think was, *We're broke. What will my friends think? My poor mom!* I needed to escape, and I was glad my summer trip to visit my dad and stepmom had arrived as a diversion.

Six weeks later, I returned home and my mom picked me up at LAX airport. As we were pulling into the driveway, I noticed a ladder. It looked like the painting of the house was underway. I said, "Mom, this is great. You got someone to paint the house!" In my mind,

painting meant there must be money, that something had changed and something positive was happening.

I was wrong. She said, "No, Hilary. *I'm* painting the house."

Mom was painting the house? She had to be kidding. "What are you talking about? *You* can't paint the house!" *What are our neighbors and friends going to think? This has to be a joke, right?* I started laughing. "Mom, you don't even know how to paint. How are you planning to do it?"

She just shrugged. "Well, I'm learning. I'm painting it with a brush, one stroke at a time."

My chin hit the floor. This sounded crazy to me. In our neighborhood, if somebody painted their house, crews arrived in trucks and teams of men in white overalls climbed up ladders and scaffolds and just took care of it. Nobody's mother got up on a ladder, much less painted the outside of their house! How was this even happening?

As you are reading this, you are probably thinking, "What a spoiled girl"—and you are right. I have to admit, I did not even volunteer to help. And Mom did not ask. I am not at all proud of this part of the story.

I would come home from school, and one more little section would be done each day. I thought for sure Mom would be humiliated, but that wasn't the case. In fact, I watched her take pride in what she was doing.

Mom worked on one small patch at a time, and by the time she finished the front of the house a year later, it was literally like she had gone through the stages of metamorphosis and emerged a butterfly—an accomplished, strong, powerhouse of a woman. She kept at it, and at the two-year mark, she finished painting the house. The big brown house now stood proud, crisp, and white, a credit to its neighborhood—but even more to the one woman who did it.

But just as she finished painting the house, we had to sell it because we couldn't afford it anymore. Years later, I asked my mom how she felt about selling the house after working so hard to make it look good, and she said, "Hilary, it wasn't the fact I painted the house that really mattered; it was the fact I finished the job." Mic drop!

I have never respected my mom more. She didn't care what her friends up the road thought, or about her status in the community, even though she was the former president of the women's auxiliary at the country club. She did not feel anything was beneath her. I had no idea the strength my mom had until she painted that house. It was her Mt. Everest, and she had ascended it on her own by mastering "the flip" of the story. The concept of flipping the story from negative to positive, which I first saw in action with my mom, has stayed with me

as a pillar of the ReLaunch process and is the genesis of the ReLaunch Flip—flip the script and watch what happens.

I was ashamed and humbled by my attitude, but this situation taught me the most incredible life lesson. Her rational mind would have told my mom—and most people—that painting this house was not feasible. But by leading with her ultra-determined heart, Mom flipped the story. Turning a potential negative into a positive, she brought such dignity to the situation. Looking back, I realized I had been witnessing a master class in showing up as your Higher Self. It's truly amazing how even the most challenging transitions can lead you through change to triumph. The Heart, Head, and Higher Self, the 3HQ™, have become a constant theme in my personal and business life.

> "If you don't like something, *change it.*
>
> If you can't change it, *change your attitude.*"
>
> MAYA ANGELOU

When we can get out of our rational minds—our heads (as in, *I can't do something or shouldn't do something*)—and tap into our Higher Selves, we open the path to manifesting the things we desire. And, in turn, those things lead us to other things: further goals and the next level of transformation.

In October 2021, several key apps on the Internet experienced a massive global outage. Disaster! The catastrophe I refer to here is not the global power grid necessary for human survival going down, but popular life-support social media including Facebook (all 3.5 billion users), WhatsApp, and Instagram going out for hours (Associated Press, 2021). Still, people panicked. Indeed, *Vogue* referred to this as "[s]urviving … offline purgatory" (Smith, 2021).

Suddenly, major communications networks screeched to a halt, and both individuals and businesses immediately started freaking out—"What am I supposed to do now?"—because we are fully aware of the role our computers, cell phones, and technology play in our lives. Each device and app plays a key role in the network of our lives and businesses and, without them,

we become communication-disabled. This paralysis proved to us, while everyone may feel connected, without our technology ball and chain, we are, in fact, dismally disconnected (Stevenson, 2018).

We may not be conscious of it, but the three Hs has a functional parallel of sorts. When the three Hs—the Heart, the Head, and the Higher Self—are connected, your 3HQ™ opens the pathways that allow you to connect to others.

Do you ever feel stuck, paralyzed, or indecisive? Maybe you're being held back by roadblocks at the head level. Without a balance of all three Hs, it's difficult to reach our full potential.

Jim Fortin, a master transformation coach, says in *The* ReLaunch *Podcast*:

> *We're never stuck. It's our thinking that is stuck. So anytime we get stuck in life, it's because we're out of options. Many times, we're going into what I call resignation as opposed to going into possibility. So, we'll hit a wall. But you're never in a bind; you're simply out of creative ways to think differently.*

Looking back, I realize my mom was able to transform the house singlehandedly. Not because she was a talented painter, but because she had a natural synthesis of the 3HQ™ developed over her lifetime.

She got out of her head by not thinking about what the neighbors might think or about finding another affordable way to get the house painted. Her head recognized she had a job to do, her heart told her she had everything inside herself to do it, and her empowering beliefs gave her the confidence to get the job done. She summoned the commitment and determination within her that brought her Higher Self to the forefront. She had a sense of purpose. Instead of feeling hopeless at the size of the job, she took it one small step at a time. Award-winning entrepreneur and speaker Nicole Bianchi calls these a series of "one small, brave move at a time" (Bianchi, 2021). It's the purposefulness of it that inspires any of us to be brave.

Oprah Winfrey has shone a bright spotlight on incorporating a sense of purpose and meaning in what we do. "You're happiest when you're productive, checking off tasks one by one. But the daily grind can eat away your sense of purpose," she has commented. In her *Queen Sugar* podcast, she notes a sense of purpose can elevate our higher selves and transform us from what she calls "a deflated doer" to a motivated person with momentum in the sails.

This is not always a quick and easy path, even for trained professionals, so don't feel discouraged if you find you need time to sort things out and find your way. Transformational ReLaunches are always a big topic on my podcast, and when I asked one recent guest, CEO development strategist Kelly Ruta, how long her own path to transformation took, she answered, "Decades." Formerly a trained physiotherapist, Ruta spent over twenty years in her field, a direct result of trying to work through her own childhood experiences.

I asked Ruta on *The* ReLaunch *Podcast* how we can all try to find a better version of ourselves and not have to wait decades with those small steps. She responded:

> *For starters, it can be tempting to try and rush on to the next thing in an effort to find your better self. For example, once you decide to look for a new job, the uncertainty may lead you to take the first offer that comes your way. If this sounds like you, you're not alone. Our culture tells us to skip over the journey and focus solely on the arrival.*

You can't rush painting a house; life is not about racing through a day, a month, or a year, but about slowing down enough to take stock of where we are on the journey.

Questions to Think About:

1. How does it physically feel when your intuition kicks in?
2. Would you consider yourself a "deflated doer" or a "person with momentum"? Both are achievement-oriented, so how do you see the difference?
3. ReLaunches are a lifelong process. Can you identify your three major successful ReLaunches? What did they have in common? Which led you to the most success, and why?

CHAPTER TWO

MOVES FOR THE SOUL

We are constantly transitioning. As my mom used to say, "Nothing stays the same. How boring would that be?" In order to make a transition, at some point, our inner selves have to catch up with where we are going. When I was growing up, we were constantly moving. I lived in eight homes by the time I was in college, and I learned major life lessons from each of them, but perhaps the greatest influence was the earliest.

At my first house, 7 Crest, I had a pretty pink bedroom all to myself, which I adored—until strangers broke in and stole all my mom's jewelry and many of the valuables in the house. We were, fortunately, away for the weekend, visiting family in Lake Tahoe.

I was four years old. We were sitting at the table having breakfast when the phone rang. I was wearing my favorite tattered, floor-length pale-blue nightgown with a Disney princess on it. My uncle handed the phone to my mom, and I saw her face turn white. I remember just looking at her and thinking, *What's wrong? Something really bad happened!* She hung up and left the room. When she came back, she said, "There's been a robbery."

I could hear the grown-ups talking about it. The burglars had come into the house through the space where the bedroom air conditioner was attached to the wall next to my window. And I remember thinking, *It was right next to my bed.* Images flashed through my mind of horrible men with masks on their faces and knapsacks on their backs crawling through this opening. I imagined them in my mom's room, right next to mine, and the box that had all the jewelry her parents had given her and all her valuables, including her wedding ring.

I remember the entire three-hour drive home, going back down from the mountains and just running through the scenario in my head of what had happened. When I got home, instead of the air conditioning unit in the pink wall, a piece of cardboard blocked the hole where they broke in.

I couldn't sleep in my bed anymore. I wanted to be anywhere but that room. It no longer had this little girl magic to it; it became very frightening and very dark. Nights were hard for me, and sleep was a struggle, with constant nightmares keeping me awake. I got into a habit of sneaking into my brother's room and sleeping in his chair, then quietly going back to my room in the early morning before he knew I had been there. I did that until sixth grade.

From a child's point of view, the robbery was terrifying. Even at age four, I could process beloved and valued things had vanished. But what my mom taught me—through daily hugs, unexpected acts of kindness, and her constant support—was that it wasn't about the things the robbers took; it was about what we had. The heart, our family love, our center were most important, and that couldn't be stolen by anyone.

Later, as a student of psychology and neuroscience, I learned fear is based on our own limiting beliefs that create events that have yet to happen. Just as my mother flipped the impact of the robbery, teaching me you can't live in fear, you can't live with thoughts of something yet to happen or that might happen in the future. My mom was not a psychologist by any means, but she set me on a path of strength and self-reliance, flipping the scary robbery incident on its head. I've often thought back on this in my work, and I have been inspired yet again by her actions.

Next, we moved to 28 Little Wood. My mom had just gotten remarried, and it wasn't *The Brady Bunch*; my new teenaged stepbrother and stepsister were typical teenagers and not exactly welcoming to their new stepmom. Sadly, within a year of moving into our joint house, my stepbrother would begin a ten-year battle with Hodgkin's lymphoma. Disregarding their history, mom stepped in as the caregiver and took my stepbrother every day to Palo Alto, a one- to two-hour drive each way, to get his chemotherapy treatments. And, once again, she did that with Heart and Head, working together with her Higher Self, her 3HQ™ propelling past the hurt feelings she had once had to a feeling of purpose—this time, a hope for survival.

After the house was painted, we had to downsize into a two-bedroom apartment. I was in eleventh grade by then, and my room was a loft with no walls—a design quirk I did not exactly welcome. Here I was, a high school teenager, and my room was open to the downstairs. I would learn another valuable lesson: when you put up walls, you also lose the sense of being open and vulnerable. One afternoon, hanging over the edge of my loft room after a phone call, I told my mom, "This is terrible. You can hear every word I'm saying!"

I can hear her voice now as she said, "Well, if you feel you really want to talk and be in private, go into the bathroom. That's where you do private things." She never allowed me to feel sorry for myself. She always pointed out that without the limits of walls, I actually had more space. Again, she flipped the viewpoint.

The next apartment was even smaller, but the lessons even bigger. I remember coming home from college and thinking to myself as I walked through the doors of the Century City apartment, *Wow, it's so small. It's even smaller than before!* The first thing mom said was, "Come over to this window." And through a tiny sliver, I could see buildings twinkling

off in the distance, a small slice of view. She commented, "Isn't it beautiful?" She took the smallest of small and made it as big as possible. With that apartment, she taught the size of something doesn't matter; it's the feelings you have behind it, the emotions that can make it expand into so much more. With each move we made, my mom leaned into her emotions and feelings, teaching me that your perspective can create your reality. A tiny window can become a big view for the person who is open to it.

Perception Is Reality

It's amazing how a random remark can make a lifetime impact—positive or negative. Graduation day was approaching at the private prep school I attended when a best friend and I, both seniors, were standing in the courtyard, excited about getting into college. We were going to the University of Colorado in Boulder! The principal turned to us and said, "I've never known anyone who actually graduated from the University of Colorado." I dismissed it as a joke. But to my friend, it was a gut punch—a snarky, negative comment with a hidden meaning she internalized as, "You aren't good enough to get into an Ivy school, or one of the better schools." She was devastated, and this feeling stayed with her into adulthood; meanwhile, I could barely remember the incident until recently when she brought it up.

We were two girls who heard the same comment yet took it completely differently. Trauma is as you see it. Your interpretation may not be the same as someone else's, even if both of you are in the exact same environment hearing the same words. It's a cascade effect. Our past situations and experiences create thoughts, then those feelings and thoughts are repeated by triggering experiences over time, formulating our beliefs about ourselves and our world.

The subconscious brain will do everything to make us stick with that familiar impression. To our brains, everything is black or white and never grey. Our beliefs are always right, factual, the last word, the done deal. It's not easy to argue with your mind. Right or wrong, it doesn't play favorites, and most of the time, it's going to win. That's where the heart comes in.

Princess Diana is an icon who, with all her obvious advantages, carried a negative, lifelong belief about life stemming from having been abandoned by her mother at age seven, when Frances Spencer divorced her husband and left the family home.

Married at barely twenty, Diana held onto her outsider insecurities, as well as her defensive nurturing instincts, for the rest of her life. Expectations for her were not high, and in school she won her only award for hamster care. Struggling academically, she did not pass any of her advanced high school exams, and she was known to refer to herself as "thick as a plank," meaning not very bright, with "a brain the size of a pea." In her brief pre-marriage work, she was a nanny and a nursery school assistant. Transforming to the famous princess, Diana flipped her insecurities by devoting herself both personally and as a member of the royal family to children and underrepresented people. She became the first member of the British royal family to publicly hug an AIDS victim, then a highly risky and controversial action.

Her life was a spectacular example of the power of the heart to affect a powerhouse transformation. Diana's heart took the lead and took her from a hamster caretaker and nursery school assistant to a global icon. Her marriage to Prince Charles may have made her a princess and, rationally, that should have been the jewel in her crown, but it was not. In fact, post-divorce, even without a crown, she flipped the script. Charles made her a princess. But that is not what made Diana Spencer the *people's* princess. As she was famously quoted saying in *The New York Times*, "I don't go by a rulebook. I lead from the heart, not the head." We all share in the duality of our outward visible selves versus what can be masked under the surface. During her famous *Panorama* tell-all interview on British TV, Diana showed that Diana the Victim—sitting with downcast eyes, smudged eye makeup, and clothes of mourning black—was never far from the spotlight as well.

No one is aligned in their 3HQ™ 100 percent of the time. The scales are constantly recalibrating. Sometimes the head takes the lead; other times, it's the heart. At times, the duality is in conflict, while at other times the 3HQ™ is in alignment with the Heart and Head as they act in concert, eliciting the Higher Self. It's up to us to monitor and address the balance of power and our emotions as we experience them. This requires a level of self-awareness that's not easy to achieve. With Diana, for instance, the switchback was so extreme. Sally Bedell Smith's biography, *Diana in Search of Herself,* related that she was referred to by a friend as "like a split personality." Diana appears to have tried to control her emotions via what evolved to be an eating disorder. Weight fluctuations and bulimia nervosa, which she spoke of in interviews, have been traced back to efforts of trying to gain a sense of control (Mitchell, 2020; Eating Disorder Hope, 2021). Self-awareness and an understanding of our behavior and emotions are the first steps to achieving the balance necessary to overcoming deep-seeded issues, eliminating recurring beliefs and the emotions tied to them, and moving forward.

Whether you are a princess, a rocket scientist, or simply *you,* your early challenges over time mold your unconscious into the hidden belief system inside your head. In reaching for balance, we must seek mindfulness of the duality of our outward, visible selves versus what can be hidden—even from ourselves—beneath the surface. We need to be mindful that we turn our perceptions into our reality.

Rebounding from Trauma

Trauma comes in all shapes, forms, and sizes, but when it enters the brain, it becomes deeply embedded because it is like an endless loop that plays over and over in the mind, triggering a response whenever there is a reminder. In my coaching business I see this with many clients in midlife, around forty to fifty, where the psychological cement has mostly hardened.

In the midst of the daily to-do list, how often do you find yourself thinking about your childhood? Not often? Maybe not—on the surface. But lying beneath lurks a different story. I frequently journey with my clients back to their childhood to find the source of some critical

beliefs. As I am the first to illustrate, our parents' voices echo in our hearts and minds—for better or worse—for decades.

Indeed, many people who have experienced childhood trauma don't even realize something was, in fact, "trauma," or they choose to forget it, shutting the door in its face. However, the body remembers trauma, even if the mind might suppress it. According to Bellevue Christian Counseling:

> *Although memories can be "forgotten" in our minds, the body remembers. Many victims of childhood trauma will experience physical symptoms and health*

issues that cannot be explained by typical ailments. When we go through trauma, our body kicks into overdrive in order to protect our lives, and when we do not work through the trauma, our body can continue to live in a state of preparation for fighting, fleeing, or freezing. Long-term stress can wreak havoc on our health. It's very likely you or someone you know has experienced trauma by adulthood (Bellevue Christian Counseling, 2016).

Recent CDC research reveals 60 percent of adults say they have suffered some sort of childhood trauma, ranging from physical and emotional abuse to stress-related impact (Houry, 2019).

The mission of my former business involved protecting children from the then-nascent category of digital abuse. I saw firsthand the devastating impact of such issues, focusing on online bullying of young children and the impact on their families. Today, one out of every five students report being bullied, and over 53 percent of adults report having experienced bullying at some point (Houry, 2019; PACERs, 2020). Approximately 20 percent of victims then experience some kind of mental health problems later in life, *even as late as the age of fifty* (Tzani, 2018).

Forty-two-year-old Chicagoan Joanne Lee Molinaro, known as "the Korean Vegan" (the name of her bestselling Korean vegetarian cookbook) has spoken of turning early trauma into a beautiful family legacy of culinary tradition. Almost three million social media followers have become fascinated not by her high-powered (now former) career as a formidable trial lawyer or her hobby of long-distance running, but by her mouthwateringly beautiful and delicious family legacy recipes, which are accompanied by the stories and life lessons of her childhood. The daughter of North Korean immigrants from a humble, even horrifying background—her mother almost died of starvation—she speaks of being bullied in American schools with racial slurs and telling people she was from Seoul because she was ashamed to admit her family was from North Korea.

"We all have baggage and things we can't unlearn, and I just have to learn to live with it," Molinaro says. And her way of "living with it" is via the heart—to find joy for others. Her path is to find middle ground via culinary culture—the creation of food that combines her Korean

heritage with a health-oriented, vegetarian diet. In her book, *The Korean Vegan*, Molinaro says, "What I've learned … is what really matters isn't whether the food tastes exactly the way your grandmother made it, but how it makes you feel." It's interesting when Molinaro describes her recipes, the word "taste" does not appear. Instead, we are treated to an emotional banquet:

> *They remind me of the garden in the backyard of our Skokie house, the deep wrinkles in my grandmother's hands. They remind me of my mother's perseverance, my father's laughter. They remind me of home (Molinaro, 2021).*

Now I know why every time I smell a pecan pie, it brings me back to a warm and comforting feeling of my childhood and my mom's incredible pecan pie.

When Molinaro posted her first recipe demonstration on TikTok, she did not throw in an extra ingredient but a little story about her mother "swooping in" to protect her in a convenience store. The post got over a million views in fewer than twenty-four hours. "When you get feedback in the form of hearts and likes and comments," she says, "it makes you want to do more. I know it sounds trite, but I just want to make [the world] a kinder place" (Eng, 2021).

From Surviving to Thriving

Licensed psychotherapist Star Rose Bond is another inspiring story of flipping fate from surviving trauma to thriving. During our interview on *The* ReLaunch *Podcast* in 2021, Bond shared many insightful tips.

A child of chronic instability, including alcoholism, poverty, and sexual abuse, she wound up on the streets and eventually incarcerated. Those experiences led to her focus on what was holding her back.

Once she understood she was 100 percent responsible for the life she was living, Bond began to create and cultivate the change needed to build the life she wanted. We all have the ability to reclaim our lives by taking control of our thoughts and beliefs—if we're mindful and willing to interrupt the ones that no longer serve us.

Knowing she would be a completely different person had she had a different past, Bond has found the silver lining, or "hidden gem" as she calls it, in every situation. As with Princess Diana, Bond's experiences give her the empathy, compassion, and passion needed to serve others, which is what she does today.

Now, as a trauma expert, Bond says, "You can change your trajectory for the better. When I was struggling to ReLaunch my life, I knew the only thing I had control of was the relationship between me and myself."

What was her most important realization? "In order to change courses in your own life, face yourself head-on," she advises. "Be willing to own up to your role in your life choices. Only

then you can create and cultivate change. First of all, it's time to stop relying on everything—and everyone—else outside of yourself to define you."

Star Rose Bond is a great example of *turning the invisible into the visible.* When you stop blaming where you are in life on outside influences, a shift happens. Over time, what's taking place on your *inside* gets reflected in what's showing up for you on the *outside*. That's when transformation really begins.

For the last fifteen years, Bond has been studying race, gender, and class:

> *Be humble and listen to the voices that don't look like you or come from where you come from. Open both your heart and your mind to their stories. We all still have so much to learn. It's a continuous conversation but holding that space will guide you on our own journey while honoring others.*

In this way, you can bring awareness into your everyday experience so when you think a negative thought or a repetitive self-criticism, you can intercept it and pivot in a more mindful manner.

Do you think you might have some trauma you might not have addressed?

Having experienced trauma myself as a child, I wanted to explore the issue further and help others understand trauma's long-lasting role in our lives. I invited Britt Frank, noted licensed trauma therapist, speaker, educator, and author, onto my podcast in 2021.

For some of us, a distinct incident leaves a lasting mark on our mind and body. Physical assault, natural disasters, and systemic oppression are some examples. For others, it looks a little different: an untreated childhood fear, a bad breakup, or a lie our culture tells us, one we buy into and beat ourselves up over. Regardless of your experiences, the odds are you've very likely suffered from trauma in some form.

We are not alone. An estimated 70 percent of adults in the United States have experienced a traumatic event at least once in their lives. A traumatic event is one in which an individual experiences a threat of death or serious injury to himself or others. And this threat can be real or perceived (Midwise Innovations, 2021).

"Trauma is an injury," says Frank. "If you break a leg, you'll most likely head straight to the hospital to get a cast. The cast will help the bone to heal correctly. When you treat trauma like an injury, you can take the time to feel it and then heal it."

The best and most hopeful part of our conversation was when Frank said:

> *With the right environment and the right resources, you can process trauma in a healthy way. First of all, trauma is not one-size-fits-all. Your trauma—everyone's trauma—is unique to you. Don't compare yourself to others. And realize if you think you haven't had a tragedy or other catastrophic event in your life, that doesn't mean your unrecognized trauma won't impact your well-being.*

To avoid the comparison trap—*my trauma is bigger than your trauma*—Frank suggests replacing your buts with ands. For example, instead of saying "I'm struggling with this feeling, *but* it's not as bad as it could be," try saying "I have a pretty great life, *and* I also have places where I feel pain."

Another great point Frank made is that the brain and body are connected, and it's powerful. When you are content, your body tells you so by feeling calm and relaxed. When you're nervous or upset, you get very different signals. Untreated trauma will continue to surface until it's dealt with.

I finally understood why, sometimes, after a tough week, I just felt the urge to curl up and binge-watch my favorite shows and eat a three-scoop caramel sundae.

Frank laughed at that one:

> *We've all been there. It's not healthy to do so, but there's a reason your body wants to. Instead of giving in, explore the feeling behind the desire and work on the root of why you want to make a poor choice. With practice, you'll be able to better understand your feelings, own them, and move forward in a healthy way.*

Once we access and accept our past, we can change and begin to transition to a new phase of self-awareness and gain an understanding of what has been holding us back. Are you ready to take your life in a new direction?

PAUSE AND RESET

Brandon Lucero, a technology entrepreneur, hit a period when he felt himself disconnecting with his business. He found taking an extended break connected him more deeply with his sense of purpose and Higher Self. Founder of The Video 4x Effect Methodology, Lucero was widely viewed as the leader in creating impactful and ROI-driven messaging for entrepreneurs. Yet he felt his motivation slipping. He described his early experience with trauma, which helped him uncover his hidden beliefs about himself so he could move forward with his transformation:

> *As a kid, I would be picked on by two older girls who were my neighbors. They would make fun of my clothes as I walked home, and the clothes I wore were clothes I loved. They were clothes I'd picked out with my mom. I still remember the clothes brand was called*

Top Dawg, and the girls would make fun of it, call me a dog, etcetera. One day, at age ten, I came home crying, and my mom asked why. I told her, and she talked to their parents and it stopped.

Nonetheless, many years later, as an adult and a professional, I always took it very personally when haters would say things on my content. Especially when my content is me. I would remember being proud, happy, and loving my clothes—and then feeling destroyed. I had to overcome those experiences in order to fully embrace who I am now with my brand and message. It's been a shedding over eight years to not be controlled by the external world for fear of being made fun of for my message.

The way I look at it, I believe your intuition—which is in your heart—is actually your Higher Self trying to communicate to you. And the way the Higher Self achieves this is not how you've been told to communicate your entire life. For instance, we've been told to look at body language, or to use spoken language. I still think there are other ways that are beyond my consciousness—and I think silence is one of the ways we communicate with ourselves, the first way to begin to listen and connect to ourselves.

I think of this as "hitting the pause button," and I see it as a necessary, perhaps even disruptive, opportunity for a reset. You might start by altering your routine in a way that works for you. This could be as simple as, on a daily basis, changing up your coffee or tea break.

Or a pause for you could mean a retreat away from it all, which I do with my clients in the spring, or by spending a few days dedicated to clearing your mind right at home a la "stay-cation" mode, or a weekend reprieve that allows you to clear out the mindset cobwebs and begin to reconnect and hear what has been on such a low volume because the other stuff is so loud.

How can you benefit from taking a pause to rethink and reflect? For many of us, this is what's needed, but we never allow ourselves to hit that pause button. In my case, an anniversary trip for five days to our favorite spot, Cabo San Lucas, gave me an opportunity to practice what I teach. I was expecting R&R, but I got so much more.

One morning, I got up early, went outside, and gave myself the time to just *be*—no talking, no texting, no emails, just a chance to observe what was coming up inside me. This awareness prompted me to grab my journal and start writing free flow. The words flew onto the pages. (Soon I realized I was actively taking myself through a process I will be sharing later in this book.) Tears that had been suppressed for years around my aging, ailing dad, parents' divorce, the feeling that I had not spent enough time with my dad when I was young, and my need to always be perfect and stoic around him caught me off guard. Erich, my husband, found me in a pile, puffy-eyed, exhausted, and needing a nap. The floodgates had opened, all because I gave it the time and attention to do so. I actually had no idea of the level and impact of trauma I had been carrying. If "pause" had brought me an awakening, a renewed energy and sense of purpose, writing in my journal had brought me a renewed sense of self—of who I really was and what I truly wanted.

It's funny how the two kinds of go hand in glove.

What is your answer to getting through some of the tough transitions in your life? When do you give yourself the gift of quiet so you can clear the noise in your head? Each of us will have a different way of accessing our innerness. You might write in your journal, as I did, or commune with nature, take a hike, play with a pet, paint, play music, exercise—whatever clears your consciousness. The white space you may encounter is waiting for you to fill it with new abundance, starting with your handwritten notes to yourself.

The Words Have It

For me, writing in my journal was the key. It might be for you as well. The actual physical connection—the line drawn from your head, where the thoughts originate, through your heart, and down through your fingers—brings all your senses into the equation. Something incredible happens when you start to write things down by hand versus typing into a keyboard.

Proven science supports this. According to Dr. Vaile Wright, senior director of healthcare innovation at the American Psychiatric Association, "Self-directed cognitive behavioral therapy—in a journal, for example—is effective at reducing symptoms of depression or anxiety" (Safronova, 2021). The pen wields a lot of power.

When I got home from Cabo, I continued the process of releasing through journaling, understanding how valuable it would be for me, as well as my relationships with my dad and my business. Everything was starting to get back in alignment, and abundance in all areas of my life suddenly became visible through the haze.

You have the power to move past your traumas, embrace your heart, appreciate your feelings, and create the awareness to not let the past hold you back. Reinventing is inside of us—the ability to realign our emotions with what is really important, turn our negative emotions into positives, and fill in our overlooked white spaces with elevated energy and opportunities.

QUESTIONS TO THINK ABOUT:

1. Have you had a moment in your past where you felt you got out of your rational mind and tapped into your Higher Self? What was the specific moment or situation? How did it make you feel? What new opportunities and possibilities were you able to tap into because of it?
2. The ReLaunch Flip involves flipping the story from negative to positive. When you are able to flip the script, even the most challenging transitions can lead you through change to triumph. Have you ever encountered a situation where you were able to do this?
3. Divide a piece of paper into two columns. On the left, make a list of situations in your life that offer challenges you might want to change. On the right, write a way you might flip the script and find an upside that might offer new opportunities.

CHAPTER THREE

LEAD WITH YOUR HEART TO CHANGE YOUR THOUGHTS

"You either walk inside your story and own it or you stand outside your story and hustle for your worthiness."

BRENÉ BROWN

In her book, *Going There*, Katie Couric writes that when she was offered the breakthrough job at CBS as the first solo female anchor of a network weekday evening newscast (for which she was paid fifteen million dollars), she "secretly wondered if [she] was really up to it." Despite her previous extraordinary career successes, Couric still felt she had to prove herself. She rationalized her way into the job by mentally positioning her achievement in light of advancement for women in general: "Proving *we* could do this." Today, she ironically asks, "Has any man in the same position ever wondered that?" (Couric, 2021). Self-esteem and your own self-worth are always tied to your beliefs, and the outside is often not a reflection of what we perceive on the inside.

Have you ever had a nagging feeling you didn't belong? I've had it many times. Looking back, it's no surprise, as I spent my childhood being shuttled between my mom's and dad's homes, a child of divorce. My parents meant well, but I just never felt 100 percent grounded in either place. Wherever I was, I always had one foot out the door. Then I was held back in first grade. Who gets held back in first grade? Clearly, I wasn't good enough. I was dumb; I was unworthy. Today, I recognize this as what would be called childhood trauma, which led to my own limiting beliefs.

Fast forward to seventh grade, an important teenage milestone. I was to deliver a three- minute Shakespeare monologue onstage—a special performance because superstar singer Helen Reddy was to be in the audience (her niece was in the class). Helen Reddy, with her feminist anthem "I Am Woman," was my heroine. I must have practiced my monologue a hundred times until I really had it down. In rehearsal, facing the huge auditorium with rows and rows of empty seats, the words flowed. But that night, I opened my mouth and nothing came out. You could have heard a pin drop.

Eventually, the drama teacher mercifully came onto the stage and escorted me off. (So much for my dream of an acting career!) This incident scarred me, and it would remain hidden in my deep subconscious. I harbored a deep-seated feeling of *I'm not good enough.* As an adult, the sharp edges of these memories faded, but my internal response was to compensate by overachieving, with the resulting success at work convincing me those feelings of inadequacy were long gone.

Or so I thought.

On a snowy day of my senior year of college, the universe stepped in to push me into what my passion and future career would bring. Due to a computer shutdown during registration, I managed to be accepted into a senior level business class, Personal Selling, despite not having completed any of the prerequisite classes.

That first day of class, I zigzagged from feeling sheer joy to feeling like I didn't belong. The teacher was telling the class we were "the elite," that from the over three hundred kids who applied, only thirty of us had gotten into this class. Still, I felt conflicted. I knew I could do the work as described in the syllabus, but the underlying, nagging fear of being unable to perform to the expectations of the teacher and the rest of the class remained. And what if I had taken the spot that should have been given to somebody else, and I failed? This class became a turning point for me. I attacked and excelled at the coursework and ultimately felt like I finally did belong, that I could be good enough sometimes. But it didn't come automatically; I had to prove it to myself over and over to verify my legitimacy.

You can run, but you can't hide. Your limiting beliefs will always rear their ugly heads and, yes, mine did reappear—years later, when as a young entrepreneur trying to launch my own business, my co-founders and I were invited to a prestigious pitch contest. This was a high- profile event where various aspiring entrepreneurs presented their business concepts to a group of potential investors, influential media, and some of the biggest names in Silicon Valley. The stakes were high, with awards, connections, and potential financing on the table.

The night before the big event, our team had a rehearsal that included me taking the stage and delivering my six-minute pitch. Walking to the podium to practice my presentation, I had a sudden sense of déjà vu. Like when I was in junior high, I found myself facing an auditorium, but this one with a thousand empty seats, including one in the front row with a sign with the name of a top *New York Times* technology reporter everyone in my industry followed and admired. Standing there, I suddenly had a massive panic attack, or should I say a massive belief attack. My hands shaking, I couldn't remember one word that only five minutes earlier I had recited flawlessly. Finally, I resorted to reading off my index card notes, fully aware that notecards were banned for the actual timed, six-minute presentation, while running one second beyond your allotted time meant automatic disqualification. This was disastrous since it was fewer than twelve hours from the start of the live event. Running into one of my employees as I left the podium, I was devastated by his look of disgust. Disaster loomed, and I had nowhere to hide.

Back at the hotel, my co-founder could only say, "Hilary, what is going on with you? I've never seen you like this." She was confused. I recognized the feeling, and it was haunting.

That thought of not belonging had embedded itself as an emotion to the point where I actually believed it—and not in a good way. As a result, I grew up with a major belief holding me back, which was that I was "not good enough." These kinds of beliefs are called "limiting beliefs" for a reason. They limit and constrict you. In my coaching, I have witnessed the resulting "not good enough" syndrome I saw plaguing so many women.

The next morning, my partner looked pale. I could tell she was really nervous about me, and she even questioned if I should back out, but I just shook my head. "I've got this." In spite of all the drama, I was able to talk myself into believing I was right where I was supposed to be, and I could do it. I made a great pitch, and we won the contest. Did I completely obliterate that unwelcome limiting belief? I wish it were that easy to talk your way into believing, but to be honest, not totally. As I had to learn later, you can will your way around a limiting belief and it may seem to have disappeared, but until you really deal with it and work through and neutralize it, a trigger can come up at any time—and anywhere—and usually it is at the most inopportune times. My feeling of unworthiness was not completely resolved until I later developed the skills to attack that limiting belief as if it were a bug that needed to be exterminated.

John Gray, PhD, author of the international bestseller *Men Are from Mars, Women Are from Venus* and twenty-some other books, explains that we basically have an evil twin:

> *If you want to manifest something in your life, you have to be willing to be able to accept it, because there's a real self and a false self. The false self feels inadequate and unworthy. And that's when you say, "I want to be the authentic self, which truly feels worthy and good enough to deserve." When you're not in touch with who you really are, you're not going to manifest what you want.*

Then, the evil twin wins.

If you are not in alignment with yourself, success is no guarantee of happiness. Even if you achieve what you want, Dr. Gray says if you're not in touch with who you are, you won't be happy.

This "good enough" syndrome is its own kind of epidemic. If you've ever felt it creeping in, you're in good company. In the article "How These Three Women Made It into the C-Suite" by Samantha Pratt Lile, leading women executives expressed variations of the "not good enough" theme. Kelly Mohr, chief financial officer of a major communications firm, says, "One of the greatest obstacles was the fear within myself I was not good enough … We can do this our way. We have strengths that are valuable and, in fact, in high demand. We need to remember that and believe in ourselves." According to the Morningstar Report, while the number of women in top tier C-level positions at Fortune 500 companies is an all-time high of forty-one, they account for only 8.2 percent of the category's CEO total (Lile, 2021).

It's not difficult to see how the "not good enough syndrome" can contribute to a cycle of self- defeatist "impostor syndrome" thinking. In fact, when it comes to what may be holding us back from our fullest potential, the three major limiting beliefs are: *I'm not good enough (worthy), I'm not safe*, and *I'm not lovable.*

Research has proven high-achieving women to be especially vulnerable (Mzumara, 2020).

I am not alone in my overcompensation response. Karen Sage, chief financial officer of a leading global software solutions company, says, "Even my fifth-grade math teacher told me I should not pursue math because I wasn't logical enough. So, what did I do with this advice? I got my undergraduate degree in math and then went on to pursue engineering" (Lile, 2021).

Impostor syndrome involves doubting your abilities and feeling like a fraud. Identified as far back as 1978 by psychologists Pauline Rose Clance and Suzanne Imes, "it disproportionately affects high-achieving people, who find it difficult to accept their accomplishments. Many question whether they're deserving of accolades" (Tulshyan and Burey, 2021).

Feeling "not good enough" holds us back from getting where we want to be; then, once we do get there, the "impostor syndrome" kicks in to try to convince us we don't really belong there. High-achieving women who share this feeling include luminous success stories ranging from Hollywood stars Charlize Theron and Viola Davis, to poet Maya Angelou, to executives former first lady Michelle Obama and Supreme Court Justice Sonia Sotomayor. So, all of us who are "not good enough" are in good company (Tulshyan and Burey, 2021). We've developed a world-class repertoire of "workarounds" where, rather than understanding and dismantling the roadblocks, we weave around them like Grand Prix drivers on the obstacle course of life.

> "And now that you don't have be perfect, you *can be good*."
>
> JOHN STEINBECK

What tools can we access to disempower a deflating mindset? Whenever I get seriously stuck on a roadblock, I like to think back to my mom's masterstroke with perspective. Maybe it's not a roadblock after all. Maybe it's an unmarked route to a beautiful view, unseen from the four- lane highway. So much of how you feel is tied to how you think about things.

Questions to Think About:

1. Do you ever find yourself doubting your self-esteem and your self-worth? Are such moments often tied to self-limiting beliefs or impostor syndrome? If so, what

are some of those beliefs and how do they make you feel? Once you've recognized those self-limiting beliefs, if they aren't true and are not serving you, are you willing to let them go?

2. What do you believe is holding you back from your highest potential? What actions can you take starting today to move forward?
3. Have you ever felt like an impostor, like you don't belong, or like you are not good/deserving enough? If so, identify some specific instances and what you might have in common with the high-achieving women in this chapter who have also shared this feeling.

PART TWO

HEAD

CHAPTER FOUR

THE RELAUNCH FLIP

I sped up the long driveway to my house, returning home after another twelve-hour day at work, still rolling over the negotiations from the manufacturing and financial systems I was selling to some of the biggest Fortune 500 companies. Business was incredible, and I wanted to grab every opportunity while it was there. With every deal I closed, my ego only grew bigger and bigger. Mom was staying with us to spend some time with the grandkids. I threw down my briefcase—yes, we still carried them then—and hurried into the family room, my adrenaline still pumping. Mom was in the kitchen, and I found myself impatiently wondering, *Where's dinner? Why was the house such a mess?* The TV was blasting from the family room. My youngest was two, and my twins were five. I was so caught up in my head, it was like I had imprinted the office on top of my house.

As I walked into the kitchen, cleaning up as I made my way through the path of destruction, I wondered why my house wasn't managed as efficiently as my team at work. I started barking out questions about the kids' day: "Mom! Did you pick up the twins from school on time? Were you able to get to the grocery store? Were you able to schedule a play date with the neighbor?"

As I blew into the kitchen, Mom turned around and looked at me with the side-eye. But I missed her clue. Finally, around the fourth rapid-fire question, Mom stopped cooking, put down the spoon, and said, "Just wait a second. Where's Hilary? Can we please have Hilary with the heart back?"

I looked at her like she was an alien. I had no idea what she was talking about. She made no sense. I asked her what she was saying. Basically, I avoided responding.

Later that night, when I went to bed, I ran through the conversation again and realized the validity in what she said. I was operating 100 percent from my Head with no room for the Heart. I had eaten the dog food of Silicon Valley, where being a pit bull (which they literally called me at work) was a good thing.

I was on target to win yet another award: the Worst Mom of the Year Award. It was a wake- up call. I did not want my kids to think of me like that. I vowed to myself to leave work at work and, when I drove up the driveway every night, I realized I had to consciously transition from Head to Heart mode.

With so many attitudes and behaviors running their own show inside of us, you might wonder how it's possible to overcome all these built-in barriers. These are internal speed bumps that can stop you in your tracks if you let them. The first step is to recognize them—or have somebody point them out to you, like my mom did—and face up to the fact they may be your ugly side. I might have done nothing that day. In fact, it can seem like a safe choice to do nothing rather than to challenge and confront the issues. Avoiding something unpleasant is much easier. So, we continue to do nothing, and history always repeats itself. However, if we do nothing, we risk becoming trapped in our heads, leaving no room for our hearts.

Looking back, I realize I could have felt like Mom was attacking me and stayed on the defensive, casting myself as a victim. But we are not victims. It's all about how we perceive ourselves. We have a choice in how we respond, then can create outcomes and determine our fate.

My name is Hilary. That's a fact. I am a female. That is a fact. If you really wrote down all the facts, there are not that many. Most of what you believe to be factual are actually not facts, but your own *beliefs*. Our behaviors are tied to who we show up as in our daily life, so if I thought of myself only as the hard-charging executive, that's who I would remain to be—unless I gave myself time to think about it and realign my beliefs about myself.

Since most of our thoughts are negative, when we hear something negative about ourselves we tend to latch onto it. For instance, to be a victim, the feeling snowballs until you start feeling horrible about yourself. The chain reaction goes like this: thoughts and emotions repeated over time create our beliefs, which, in turn, determine our behavior (Morin, 2016).

Instead of dwelling on the negative side of Mom's comments—if you think you're a failure, you'll feel like a failure—I realized I had the choice to change the outcome. I flipped a potentially negative outcome into something positive for the whole family.

As I brushed my teeth that night, I looked at myself in the mirror and wasn't proud of the image that looked back. The stress wasn't just on the inside; it was blazingly obvious on the outside as well. I looked tense, and my skin was grey. No wonder the dentist had just given me a mouth guard—I was grinding my teeth in the middle of the night. Not only did my jaw need an adjustment, but my beliefs also needed a major overhaul. This realization, which was a sparking of a heart that had been sandbagged in routine, marked a key milestone in my personal and professional development. In many ways, my journey toward my coaching career and even this book began that night.

Meet B.U.G.S. That's what I call unexamined negative beliefs that surface—Beliefs UnderGround Surfacing. When you uncover the root of your B.U.G., you have found what

client Anne Abreu, founder of She Packs Lite, coined as your "Queen Bee." This is the big one, the one who controls the nest inside your head. She has a megaphone and is shouting, "Hilary, don't forget, we failed first grade! Repeat that a million times!"

It's that simple and that complex. It's like we've set up a luxury hotel in our heads for an unwelcome Queen Bee who has somehow made herself so at home she never leaves. It's not that easy to toss her out the door and out of our lives. Why should she make it easy? She's made a lifestyle out of borrowing our favorite sweater, hogging the TV remote, messing up our Wi-Fi, leaving the dishes in the sink, not walking the dog, taking off in our car and leaving it with an empty tank, and making us feel like losers for allowing all this.

You won't usually recognize this thought pattern until Her Majesty has already claimed the slacker real estate on your mental couch. In other words, you're already stuck in a negative place. From there, you find yourself in a mindset trap.

How do you know when you're headed into this race to the bottom? Remember you *feel* like you *think*. Flip your current thoughts with those that support you instead of leading you to a place of fear.

Fear is based on the future, something that has not even happened. Usually, fear is based on a limiting belief that needs to be addressed to keep it from recurring. These B.U.G.S. simply do not pack up and leave the premises without an assist from you. With practice, you'll be able to interpret your life differently and see things from another angle. That's when others will see *you* differently.

An example of this is Terry (not her real name), a TV personality whose father ran a successful midsized accounting firm. She has vivid memories of her father coming home from work with a grim expression on his face, saying, "I've got to break the back of this thing," meaning whatever work situation he was facing. To Terry, this meant the whole family was in danger from some terrible monster that had to be wrestled to the ground, daily, by her hardworking dad.

After college, Terry's father helped her land a coveted internship at a major accounting firm. The first day on the job, she stood up on her chair. She looked over the top of her cubicle, saw dozens of other cubicles just like hers, occupied by people just like her, and her heart froze. She saw images of her father and her thoughts flashed to the lifelong sense of drudgery she felt would ultimately eat her alive. Suddenly, the B.U.G.S. were crawling all over her. She walked out and swore she would never work in an office like that again in her life. Nobody could understand how she had walked away from such a great opportunity. But for the first time, Terry realized she didn't want her destiny to be tied to becoming a drone in someone else's company. She faced her fears and took her first steps toward not just taming that

B.U.G., but becoming a successful entrepreneur with an award-winning business of her own.

Based on her childhood experiences, such as her dad constantly making what she perceived as scary comments like, "This place is going to eat me alive," Terry instinctively felt unsafe in the corporate world. She weighed her options, including the risk of not taking a sure thing, and made an informed decision that was her safest bet—i.e., get out before all hell broke loose. Perhaps the person in the next cubicle had other fears, but not the ones that would send him or her fleeing from their cubicle. Everyone's needs and fears are unique to them.

Growth never comes from standing still. Challenges always involve risks. But it's perfectly okay to challenge yourself to tackle your B.U.G.S. I love the expression that without change, there would be no butterflies. It's time to morph.

In the 1940s, psychologist Abraham Maslow established foundational research documenting that, as humans, the most common, core limiting beliefs stem from: 1) need for safety; 2) need to be loved; 3) need for self-esteem, to feel worthy and good enough (Lester, Hvezda, Sullivan, and Plourde, 1983).

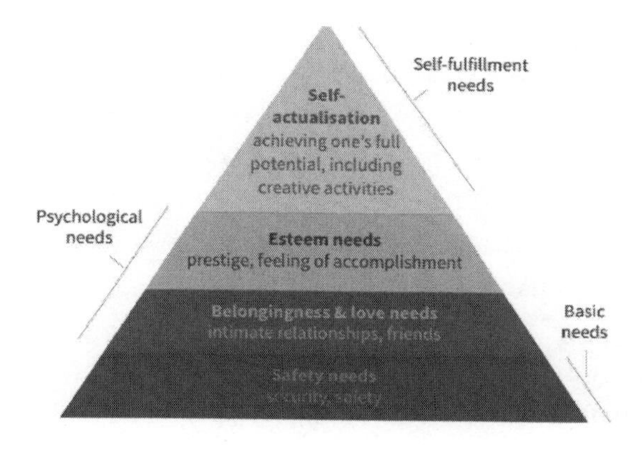

Fear is the big one. If you live in the wilderness and a huge bear runs toward you, you'd probably act much in the way that ancient predecessors did when a mastodon came charging in their direction. Today, our predators are usually of a different sort—

financial shifts, health scares, relationship issues—but many of us nonetheless live our lives in fight-or-flight mode, which shows up as a continual state of stress. It creates cortisol, which can cause numerous physical, emotional, and mental disorders—up to and including illness (Williams, 2018). For me, stress was my status quo.

Stress has become quite a buzzword these days, with good reason. It's basically unavoidable. You may not be able to control the reasons for it, but you can control your reactions to it. What if you overcame fear and stress by controlling your thoughts? What if, instead, you exerted personal power within you to change the game?

This is where fear often steps in. I would challenge you to ask yourself, *What is there to fear?* A recent study proved that 85 percent of what people fear never happens (Goewey, 2015). Who has the time for that kind of wasted energy? You can't control the future, so why not focus on controlling the controllable—managing your thoughts—and take action? (Park and Huang, 2010).

THE POWER TO CHANGE THE GAME

If fears are caused by negative beliefs, repetition of positive actions and empowering beliefs have an incredible impact. Maybe you read Malcolm Gladwell's book *Outliers* and his explanation about how ten thousand hours of repetition can elevate good to great and create a master (Gladwell, 2013). For instance, how the young, pre-fame Beatles were sentenced by a bad contract to playing dive bars in Germany that involved grinding out five shows a day for months. Between August 1960 and December 1962, the Beatles played over two hundred fifty nights in Hamburg, with venues often demanding they play four or five hours a night. It was a terrible financial deal and a physical ordeal, but it cemented their psychological bonding and their creativity as a group. Lennon said, “In Hamburg, we had to play for hours and hours on end. Every song lasted twenty minutes and had twenty solos in it ... That’s what improved the playing” (Wickman, 2012). It’s been pondered, without this level of experience, would the Beatles still have become the Beatles?

A note here. Since the publication of Gladwell’s book, in which the “ten-thousand-hour rule” was based on a 1993 study of violin students, science has evolved yet again. The premise of hours has been challenged as perhaps an overstatement (Goldhill, 2019). But nobody can deny the success of Gladwell’s examples. Talent is perhaps a component that defies quantification by science.

However, it has been scientifically documented our brains can literally be retrained physically by repetition. Many of us have seen examples of this firsthand without realizing it. For instance, repetitive therapies are a staple of post-stroke rehabilitation, retraining the brain to create new or alternative neural networks to substitute for the original connective signal paths that have been damaged or lost (Earle, 2021). And have you ever wondered how expert figure skaters are able to spin through the air without losing their balance? Mirai Nagasu, the 2018 US Olympic team bronze medalist, explains this as “a learned ability against the momentum that hits us while we’re spinning.”

Kathleen Cullen, professor of biomedical engineering at Johns Hopkins University, attributes this to the vestibular system, which is the area of the brain responsible for balance and motion. Cullen notes although athletes feel the spins happening, their brains adapt and learn to ignore the feeling of dizziness. "There's a really profound fundamental thing that happens in the brain of people like dancers or skaters over lots and lots of practice. That's basically a change in the way the brain is processing information" (Karimi, 2022). Basically, the brains of these athletes are choosing not to feel dizzy.

We *can* reprogram ourselves to act, react, and feel differently; we have choices. Choices that can impact not just our careers and relationships, but our body, spirit, and soul. What we do with these choices is up to us, but the first and most important step is realizing we have them. Competence breeds confidence. When an Olympic-level skater flies spinning over the ice in a double axel, she can feel confident she's not going to feel dizzy, which in turn impacts her overall performance and her score. They say knowledge is power, but when we operate on autopilot and don't utilize this priceless asset, it's powerless.

It's important to always be aware you are owner and CEO of You, Inc. Transformational expert Jim Fortin asserts that in most situations, even when you feel you have no control, you *can* control your thoughts. Fortin focuses on the theory of most people having one root thought that all other thoughts come from, what he calls the "master thought." If this master thought is negative, it can lead to depression, anxiety, and fear. Not surprisingly, when this thought is in control—put in the driver's seat by your subconscious—you wind up feeling trapped. But *you* have the power over your master thought, so if yours has you in its grip, Fortin has a simple solution: choose a new thought.

In fact, science has concrete evidence you can take specific actions to trigger a more desirable habit. For instance, if you want to lose weight but can't stop eating, replace junk food snacking with fruit and put the fruit in an easily accessible place far from where you kept the junk snacks. If you do this often enough, you can replace the junk food habit with a healthier one. Repetition of the new habit is the key. It doesn't happen overnight; science suggests it can take anywhere between fifteen and two hundred fifty-four days to form a new habit. If you stick with it, it can be done (Young, 2018).

Transformational leader, master life coach, best-selling author, and law of attraction expert Christy Whitman had to confront these issues herself when, a few years ago, her business suddenly shifted from making seven figures to not generating enough revenue to pay all her employees. She was torn between wanting to stay loyal to everyone within her company, holding on to what she had left as long as she could, and, at the same time, realizing she needed to make difficult internal changes in order to bring her work back in alignment with her goals.

Although her work was dedicated to helping others realize the power of manifestation, she felt the need to go deeper when applying her principles to herself. She intensified her efforts to master her own energy and direction, consulting healers and practicing healing work. "I focused on rediscovering the forgotten, ancient knowledge and spiritual wealth" (Evercoach, 2021).

Whitman was aware that, if you send out negative emotions, you will attract them in return—that until she changed, her business will also remain unchanged (Kelly, 2013). She says, "Our desires are meant to be expansive, feel good, inspirational, and joyous to create the best version of ourselves."

> "Your *imagination* is your preview of life's coming attractions."
>
> ALBERT EINSTEIN

QUESTIONS TO THINK ABOUT:

1. What walls have you put up in your life that may be limiting access to your Higher Self? What caused you to put up those walls? Are you ready to let go of and break down those walls in order to align with possibilities? What actions would you need to take, or positive beliefs would help take down those walls?
2. When do you pause to access your innerness and create white space and peace for yourself?
3. Can you find examples in your own life where you have done a "ReLaunch Flip" and shifted the viewpoint from negative to positive? What was the outcome? Is there a situation right now where you could do that?

CHAPTER FIVE

HELL IN THE HALLWAY

At age two, I was hospitalized with a serious bacterial infection called shigella. I think of that little girl and how scared she must have been going in and out of hospitals for six months. Finally, the night they said I would die, a doctor decided to try something extreme and give a massive dose of antibiotics. He said to my mom, "We have nothing to lose." The antibiotics kicked in, and a week later—at half my former body weight—I went home. As a teenager, I learned my mom had not been allowed to stay overnight with me in the hospital. This traumatic experience imprinted somewhere deep inside me because I had been too young to process it at the time. I must have pushed it down deep into my subconscious and shut it away behind a door in my mind.

Other traumas, also tucked away, followed. For instance, being told I was going to be held back in first grade, and that little girl feeling like she's dumb. Then, as I got older, my parents' divorce, the robbery, and my grandparents being killed in a car crash when I was in seventh grade. All of these incidents could have—and would have—overwhelmed a small child, tween, or adolescent with thoughts and emotions in a cascade effect. I needed to be able to listen to all of those inner girls and realize that, in order to survive, I had to put them behind doors. It was just too overwhelming for me to deal with in those younger years.

When traumatic emotional issues arose later, as an adult, I habitually left them behind the door, preferring not to deal with them and instead powering through them. "Powering through" an emotional issue is disabling because if we feel we're not strong enough to tackle these issues, we often feel like failures. As a child and young adult, I was not able to address so much trauma, but as an adult, I could. However, to be able to open the door to these traumatic events, I needed a way to process them.

In "Is 'Powering Through' Really a Good Thing?" Vanessa Torre writes, "Telling people to power through is destructive. It's revving the engine of a high-quality car into the red and expecting it to be fine. It won't be fine. Eventually even that power-filled machine is going to blow" (Torre, 2019). In fact, it's not the intensity of our efforts to just get through tough times—"where there's a will there's a way"—but an awareness that more needs to be done so things don't compound and continue to repeat in our lives. Our own self-limiting B.UG.S. block our ability to create who we ultimately want to be.

Do any of these phrases sound like the voices in your head? Do you have any of these B.U.G.S.?

- *I'm not good enough.*
- *I'm not worthy.*
- *No one is going to love me.*
- *I don't belong here.*

- *I'm not thin enough/pretty enough/smart enough.*
- *I'm too old/too young.*
- *I have no time.*
- *I don't have the money to ...*

The good news is it is possible to intercept those limiting beliefs—those B.U.G.S.—and *change the course of your neurobiology* (Talk of the Nation, 2007; Barrett, 2020).

According to neurological scans, it is possible to create a new, positive-only mindset by erasing the negativity that can affect brain health via self-generated neurochemistry. Negative thoughts stimulate the release of negative chemicals into your brain while positive, loving, or encouraging thoughts do the opposite (Amen, 2019). When you work to cultivate a new biological landscape, you can literally alter your brain and potentially change your mindset and future.

This is an analogy for how you might be dealing with your personal B.U.G.S.; a lot of your limiting beliefs are shut behind those mentally closed doors. So, you think about your divorce, and then you start to think, *Well, that was a huge failure. I'm not good enough to have a marriage that works.* Unfortunately, those pesky B.U.G.S. are opening the door a crack, slipping under, and inching out into the hallway a few at a time. Next thing you know, you are sitting across from a date, he asks about your divorce, and that door is blown wide open and an army of B.U.G.S. are swarming you. It's hell in the hallway.

Sometimes, we don't even realize we have a problem. Maybe it's so hurtful we've repressed it, hidden it behind one of those doors. Repression is a self-defense mechanism. It's easier to push things down than to confront them. But later we're in inertia mode, our comfort zone, and we wonder, *Why can't things work out for me?* We can't move forward when we don't realize why we're not moving at all (Psychology Today, 2021).

When you think about hell in the hallway, know those doors are opening up, and you're toggling between one situation, then another, then another. Toggling is not moving forward. Toggling, I believe, is moving sideways. You're kind of stepping out of the way.

Rather than toggle, *listen.* Are you listening to your inner voice? At this point, it is critical to be able to hear it through the clutter. Think of this as "Marie Kondo-ing" (the icon of "tidying up" any space) your mind; she talks about tidying up your house, but it's really your mind we need to declutter first. Silence can scare us more than being at a frenetic pace because what will you emerge as when you allow yourself to go into that hallway? You need to open those doors and listen, acknowledge your B.U.G.S., and address them.

World-renowned mindset and behavioral researcher John Assaraf talks about this process. He has had many ReLaunches in his life but feels the most impactful was his first. Coming from a family that was low on the financial resources scale, Assaraf said in our discussion on *The* ReLaunch *Podcast,* "It was easier to just shut the door—door after door—about anything I didn't like about myself and the results of my bad decisions."

Finally, at age nineteen, Assaraf found himself at a crossroads, eager to leave his troubled youth and sabotaging ways and behaviors behind. At last, he was willing to open some of those doors, realizing his choices were, as he said, "ultimately going to lead [him] either to jail or the morgue." He committed to doing whatever it took to make it to success. "If you lead with your thoughts, understand there are no valid excuses, and stay committed to your growth, you will reach your goals."

Assaraf remembers the exact day when everything changed for him. That's when his brother's colleague agreed to meet with him to see if he could help this troubled young man. He realized he had to learn to show up as the person he wanted to be, physically and emotionally.

Learning how to upgrade his thoughts, beliefs, and habits from his mentor, Assaraf created his framework for success—a mindset, skill set, and actionable set of lessons. He realized how much power the mind held and started practicing daily affirmations to eradicate his limiting beliefs and rewire his brain. "There's also a huge connection between the mind and the body, meaning what you think about will become your reality," he points out.

The first thing Assaraf's mentor did was ask him to list his goals. He named immediate ones, such as owning his own car and having the means to move out of his parents' house. Then the mentor asked Assaraf the big question: "Are you just interested in achieving your goals, or are you committed?"

If you're only focused on achieving the end goal, you miss the process it takes to get there. According to Assaraf, being committed involves telling yourself:

> *Whatever it takes, I'm going to get there and reckon with those limiting beliefs that are keeping those doors shut and your success stagnant. You'll do what's easy and convenient instead of what's life changing.*
>
> *Your commitment will help you develop the habits you need to achieve your goals. It takes consistency to reach them, but you'll be motivated to do whatever it takes—no more excuses.*

You must train your brain to release the B.U.G.S. behind your own closed doors. Assaraf believes you can override this. Check your mindset, match your self-image with your vision and goals. This will help you develop new beliefs empower you.

The enemy here is not ourselves; it's stagnation. Let's say you're poised and ready to move forward. Sounds like a great idea. You're all in! But how to start? How about starting small? Don't try to blast all your B.U.G.S. at once. Clearing the hell in the hallway is not an overhaul; it's a steady drip. Start with one of the doors and really think about one of those impactful moments in your own history, then go forward from there.

In his bestselling book *Tiny Habits: The Small Changes That Change Everything*, world- renowned behavior scientist and author B. J. Fogg of Stanford University suggests small and simple changes can lead to habits that last and, in turn, to behavioral shifts (Godoy, 2021).

Nicole Bianchi calls these a series of "one small, brave move at a time" (Bianchi, 2021). To me, Bianchi's use of the words "small" and "brave" in the same breath is truly inspiring, because we often find it can take more courage to make that first tiny move out of the "safety circle" of the familiar than to make a larger step—not unlike my mom painting the house one brushstroke at a time. The first step is the icebreaker on that ReLaunch journey. Does it take guts to start? You bet. Is it worth it? It will be.

Click! The door is unlocked and opening through our own self-awareness. And with each small action or step, the possibilities and the options that are there will become one step closer.

QUESTIONS TO THINK ABOUT:

1. Think about choices. Online, find a copy of Robert Frost's timeless poem, "The Road Not Taken." Can you apply the thoughts in this poem to your own life? What's your "road not taken?" Is it time to get out of your comfort zone?
2. What choices are you now facing? These are options for your life today. How will your decisions impact your life going forward?
3. What B.U.G.S. are showing up in your thoughts? What is one step you could take this week to deal with one of these beliefs to blast it from your thoughts? What is your current Queen Bee? What thought that is serving your

highest and best self can you replace it with? How would that impact your life?

CHAPTER SIX

B.U.G.S. BE GONE

The feeling of not being "good enough" can show itself in many ways, but a surprising number of women share a common fear. For almost half of all women, fear of failing and being left broke can be the Queen B.U.G.

My friend Liz was at an elite-level forum where Gloria Steinem was leading a discussion on women's finances. Ms. Steinem was clearly a role model to those in the room. Everyone assumed she would talk about her commitment to feminism. Instead, she began with a story about her greatest fear, which was to end up a bag lady. Ms. Steinem asked if anyone in the audience also feared they might become a bag lady—shuffling along, pushing a shopping cart filled with all their worldly possessions—and about a third of the room raised their hands. "I was always sure I would end up as a bag lady," Ms. Steinem said. "A fear I handled by thinking, *It's a life like any other. I'll just organize the other bag ladies*" (Tisdale, 2021).

This is such a common B.U.G. among women that it has a name: Bag Lady Syndrome (Ruef-Lindquist, 2021). A 2013 survey conducted by Allianz, a financial services company, revealed "46 percent of respondents said they harbored a 'tremendous fear of becoming a bag lady.'" The number was even higher—48 percent—among women with an annual income of more than $100,000. Further, one third of women who earn $200,000 or more also worry about becoming a bag lady (Toller, 2007). Don't you wonder how fear of failure can even exist in the same sentence as *PhD*, *clinical psychologist*, and *four published books?* These limiting beliefs can be frighteningly counterintuitive. Dr. Melissa Bird, PhD, a self-described "kick-ass" clinical psychologist, admits in *The* ReLaunch *Podcast* to a defeatist attitude that overcame her in the middle of writing one of her books: "I remember climbing from the bottom to the top of the stairs, unable to even look at my husband, thinking, *I'm so afraid I'm going to fail and we'll be living in a cardboard box.*" Dr. Bird's fears of homelessness spiraling into her relationship with her husband is an example of the domino effect of these emotions once they have cemented into beliefs.

Even Oprah, one of the wealthiest women in the world, is not immune. She has spoken candidly about the fact she has fifty million dollars in cash "stashed away in her 'bag-lady fund'" (Seegert, 2017; Toller, 2007).

Clinical psychologists like Nancy Molitor, PhD, have traced this fear largely back to childhood (Seegert, 2017). This resonates with me because my own secret, scary B.U.G. is sliding down the economic scale, as I witnessed with my mom and stepdad when he lost his job.

An interesting note here is, as Suze Orman—an American financial advisor, author, and podcast host—points out, "We never hear the phrase '*bag man syndrome.*' On some level, all women have this fear what they have will be taken away from them" (Toller, 2007). When I hear this, I think of the robbers in my childhood room, and the fear they might have stolen not only jewelry, but … me.

As my experience highlights, the impact of a B.U.G. can resonate in a ripple effect through the decades. One leading CEO told me a story of a life-changing incident that occurred when he was a ten-year-old child. "I was walking into the classroom, and the teacher announced, 'We are going to do presentations today,'" he said. When the teacher called him to be the first presenter:

> *I got up to the front of the classroom, and as soon as I opened my mouth, the entire class started cracking up, laughing at me. My best friend was laughing louder than anybody in the group. He was pointing at my pants, and I looked down and saw that my zipper was open. I was so humiliated! I ran from the classroom. I ran down the hall and into the boys' bathroom. The teacher and the boys actually chased me down the hall and followed me into the bathroom.*

He continued the story and said he looked at himself in the mirror later that day at home and told himself:

> *I can't let this happen again. I'm going to make sure my clothes are perfect. My hair is perfect. Everything I do will be perfect. [I started getting amazing grades] because that separated me from everybody else, but it created this perfectionism block I carried for forty*

years, until my business partner said to me one day when I became the CEO, "You know you're a perfectionist. That's an emotional block." I said, "Okay." Then he said, "Has it ever stopped you?"

This man, now a significant leader in his community and business, went to college, got married, had kids, and forgot all about the incident. However, every time he got angry, he jumped into overdrive perfectionism mode. Overcompensation had become his conditioned response. He realized his partner was right; he had an emotional block.

Therapist Kim Ward, PhD, has noted the recollection of childhood traumas is a kind of self- sabotage that can lead to giving up before you even try. You automatically imagine a negative outcome—even if you have long forgotten the event. This CEO's humiliation was on repeat inside his heart and his head, subconsciously reinforcing and reconfirming the perfectionist habit and validating the beliefs. It then becomes truth (Ward, 2020).

A truly 3HQ™ ReLaunch is about mindset and mindfulness—being aware and making conscious choices, becoming who you want to be and were meant to be, and closing the gap from where you are now to get there. Along the way, you must blast those B.U.G.S. that get in the way into psychological roadkill.

To Get a Reaction, You Must Take Action

Each phase in the 3HQ™ Method prepares and primes us for the next. For instance, before you can gain traction in your quest to ReLaunch, you must first identify and understand what your B.U.G.S. are. Ask yourself, *Do I have any relationship B.U.G.S. hanging around in my hallway?* For me, it was a matter of where did I *not* have B.U.G.S. Work, for sure, but I always felt my competitive nature would ultimately beat them back. Relationships, however, were another matter. Here, spreadsheets or quarterly reports can't show success.

After an unexpected divorce and years of being in and out of relationships, I decided to forget about scrolling through the dating sites like Chemistry and Match, and I went for my B.U.G.S. first. I blasted those negative beliefs so I could start fresh. I decided to work on a few of my very sticky relationship B.U.G.S., kick them off the couch, out the door, and out of my life. I had all the excuses:

"All the good ones seem to be married. Are there any great guys left?"

"Between work and kids, I have no time to meet a guy."

"I am getting older by the second, and I need to find a guy when I'm still young."

Rather than call in the exterminator, I decided to become one.

Are you ready to go for it—confront the limiting beliefs that have been holding you back, then blast your B.U.G.S. to clear the way to ReLaunch? This five-step "Belief Blaster™" is an exercise I created to guide myself—and now you—through the process. This is a multipurpose exercise that works for relationships, but also for business. Most importantly, it will get you started—a first step in exorcising your own B.U.G.S. Once you have aligned your Heart and Head, pay attention to your intuition, which may now emerge and punch you in the gut, telling you it's time to flip the script and ReLaunch now.

BELIEF BLASTER™ EXERCISE

The most common limiting beliefs funnel into not feeling safe, not feeling loved, or not feeling worthy/good enough, and can sound like:

- I'm not smart enough
- I'm not pretty enough
- I'm too old / young
- I don't have enough time
- I never do anything right
- I don't have enough money

STEP 1: REALIZE 

Realize that you have a limiting belief by recognizing your negative thoughts. Realize that wherever you lack something important in your life there is a reason and you need to uncover it.

Look to where in your life this belief has shown up before and *write it down.* Rewind your life backwards in decades. If you are in your forties, where did you see this limiting belief validated? Where did it show up in your thirties? Keep writing until you get all the way to when you can first remember this limiting belief. End up at 0-10 years of age.

With each mention, ask yourself: "How did this limiting belief make me feel?" What emotions are coming up around the limiting belief and the situations you are remembering? Notice the emotions that keep coming up and write them down. Circle the common ones that you repeated the most.

STEP 2: AWARENESS 

In this Step, you need to take the Realize Process above and keep going with it. Recall all the times that this limiting belief was NOT actually true. Because if you can remember even one time then it is no longer a fact and you can blast it. Remember that a limiting belief is one that you believe one hundred percent true one hundred percent of the time.

Take your belief back through the decades and *write down an opposite time where something happened during those years that was a positive and would negate your limiting belief:*

> ***Example:*** *I'm not good enough. Instead, change it to "I am good enough." Where have you seen this in your life?*

STEP 3: RELEASE 

It is critical to take a moment to reflect and ask yourself where you think this belief came from. Is it your belief, or was it somebody else's? Perhaps it started with your parents, a teacher, or a friend. Can you recall an actual person? We are not looking at placing blame on them but to understand that it was not your belief and that you have over the years taken it on as your own. Once you have identified the genesis of the belief with neutral feelings about it, you can choose one or both of the processes below. I have found they both work independently, but a double punch really blasts it and gives you more opportunity to activate different areas of your brain.

Option A Part 1: Write a theoretical release letter to the person who created this belief within you. Make a heartfelt letter, and explain how you really feel. You should release the belief because it is not serving you. End the letter by forgiving them and acknowledging it is no ones fault but it is time to release it and create a new empowering belief.

Option A Part 2: Create a theoretical letter that you will receive in return from the person above. Say whatever your heart needs to hear and feel. The subconscious does not know whether things are true or false, it will believe this letter is true. You now release self-sabotage and begin your journey forward.

(Modified from John Gray, The Feeling Letter, 1984).

Option B: Think of someone you love and repeat your limiting belief out loud for 30 seconds to 2 minutes, visualizing speaking to them. This allows you to tell your loved one what you say internally to yourself. This triggers the emotional part of the brain (the right side) to help release the belief from not just the logical side but also the emotional side.

(This is based on Dr. Shannon Irvine's mirroring step in The Mind Matrix™ 2018).

STEP 4: RELAUNCH FLIP™ 

Do a ReLaunch Flip™ and convert your limiting belief into a positive statement. For instance, a limiting belief might be: "I need to work hard for success." Flipping the script would be: "Success comes easily to me". Do not use any negative words in your affirmation, as the subconscious does not differentiate between negatives and positives.

Write down as many positive statements as you can (10-20 is a good goal). These are your new affirmations. It is important to be affirming what you are saying to your mind with what you want; your mind does not know the difference between an inner voice or an outer one. Create a visual movie around your belief that your affirmation is true and make sure to include how you would show up and feel. You are now firing different areas of the brain—and, again, what you see in your mind's eye is as important as you see with your two real eyes.

STEP 5: RETRAIN YOUR BRAIN 

Part 1: *Put those affirmations from Step 4 into a voice recording APP* (I love Think UP). Record these affirmations as if they have already happened. Put the emotion behind your voice with excitement that this is already done and true. Listen to this for 5 minutes, 3 times a day.

Part 2: When you wake up, *look yourself in the eye in the mirror* and repeat the mantra below:

RELAUNCH MANTRA

I love you, (your name).
Be me, Do me, Have me back.
I love me (hand gesture).
I love me (hand gesture).
I love me (hand gesture).

HAND GESTURE:  + 

Repeat this process for 62-67 days to create new neural pathways and new positive beliefs. Your limiting belief has literally been broken apart like a fractured link in a chain. The new, empowering belief has taken over. If you stop before you have completed the 62-67 days, you will fall back into your prior limiting beliefs so keep this process going.

Congratulations on eliminating your first B.U.G. through the Belief Blaster™!

QUESTIONS TO THINK ABOUT:

1. Are you a human power mower, "powering through" certain issues in your life? Identify one or more situations that result from powering through instead of fully dealing with and examining the issues. What would be a better approach for the future?
2. What is something you found yourself "toggling"? If you were to hit pause, how or what would your intuition tell you to do?
3. What is a small or simple habit you will commit to starting and forming this week that will help you get closer to your goals?

CHAPTER SEVEN

INTUITION INTERCEPTIONS

Let's just say intuition doesn't show up too often on a business plan, and nobody has figured out a bulletproof way to monetize it for investors. But for over two decades, I've always believed one of the secret weapons of my coaching business was my intuition. I would get a strong, intuitive sense of what direction people should go in their business and relationships, especially the one with themselves, and I was able to lead them to uncover their truths. It's interesting how, although I had this amazing gift with others, I chose to not listen when it had to do with my own life, and especially my business.

An August 10, 2018, article by Tibi Puiu exploring the role of instinct in decision-making in *ZME Science* reported that it's estimated decisions made by intuition alone are accurate more than 90 percent of the time.

Maybe it's the vocabulary. "Intuition" is an emotionally charged word, especially in a gender- biased sense, where the term is weighted toward women—the idea of "women's intuition" is commonplace, but who says "men's intuition?" (Riggio, 2011). It's interesting that when described as a "gut feel"—which basically amounts to intuition—intuition gets a much warmer reception from business leaders. For instance, when making the most important decision of his career—the $5.4 billion acquisition of Princess Cruises—the CEO of Carnival commented, "I trusted my gut" (Maidique, 2011).

In fact, intuition can show up in different ways. For some, it's a "gut feel." For me, it's often a whole-body sensation—maybe a tingling, or hair on my neck standing on end. For you, intuition might appear as simply "knowing" or "feeling." The key is to train yourself to recognize and acknowledge your intuitive sense. When interacting with your 3HQ™, this can be the accelerator that boosts you into taking the action to transform.

Are you ready to say *yes* to your inner voice, to give yourself the intuitive advantage that just might make a difference in a critical outcome? Kim Woods, an intuitive business strategist who worked with me during my nine-plus years at Oracle and helped me to level up my intuition, says, "Your first step is to trust your intuition. It's important to know in this world, you're trained to ignore your intuition. However, if you don't have this imperative piece of yourself, you can't get to the other parts."

Kim advises to start by asking yourself simple questions: *Should I bring that umbrella with me today?* Or, with higher stakes: *Does this conversation feel safe?* Then go with your initial answer. Practice on the smaller questions before going big. Questions such as: *Should I leave my job?* or *Should I marry this person?* should come after you start learning to use your intuition regularly. "Practice is what gives the brain a shot at mobility, at learning new things," she says. "It's no different when it comes to intuition. Once you learn to recognize it, you can hone it" (Peak Wellbeing, 2016).

In a September 30, 2019, article in *INC*, Marla Tabaka noted the iconic entrepreneurs who are known to have relied on their intuitive senses, including Steve Jobs and Richard Branson. As Jobs said, "Have the courage to follow your heart and intuition. They somehow already know what you truly want to become. Everything else is secondary."

In my coaching work, I've found one of the biggest barriers to women moving forward is lack of trust in their own intuition, which could be the gateway to connecting to their inner selves, their emotions, and the wider universe of truth.

In fact, it's easy to dismiss intuition as happenstance, or random consequences, when it is proved right. But what if it's proved *wrong*? "I trusted my intuition, and I got it wrong!" As a result, the fallback is this person refusing to trust their intuition in the future. Has this happened to you? Have you considered your interpretation of the situation was wrong? You interpreted it to mean one thing, but it was actually something else; you were just blocked to the reality. Your intuition was leading you down a path to a lesson you had to learn in order to grow, but you didn't want to hear. It is now time to pay attention.

So much of life is about not only the outcome, but the lessons learned along the way.

Tipping Points/Flipping Points

Brandon Lucero went from $40,000 in debt to owning a multimillion-dollar business in two years. Yet, without a sense of inner alignment, his vision faltered. I asked Lucero about it:

> *You have to be 100 percent aligned with what you're doing. And I've had to battle a lot of things. Even when I was selling YouTube courses and teaching people how to produce videos that attract customers, I felt misaligned. I almost felt guilty for taking people's money because I was resenting them asking questions, I wasn't showing up to the best of my ability. And for me personally, when I felt I had that misalignment, our revenue started going down. Initially, having a five-hundred-thousand-dollar business made me feel fired up. I was excited to go teach the content and help people, and then over time, I started to feel there's something more for me. As soon as I hit that moment, my product launches started getting worse because my energy had shifted.*

During his last product launch, Lucero's attitude was basically a brush-off; *let's just get through this, make some money, and just move on.* What happened as a result? Sales were half of what he was expecting, while his energy and emotions were drained. He knew something had to change:

> *It didn't bomb, but it was one of the least-performing launches we've done in years, and it was because I didn't have the energy to show up. I wasn't coming from a place of service. My intention was in the wrong*

> *spot, and we saw that in lack of sales. My intuition was trying hard to say, "Hey, knock, knock, knock, this isn't what you're supposed to be doing."*

At this point, Lucero flipped the script for a 3HQ™ ReLaunch, shifting his emphasis onto an opportunity his earlier work had ignored—not making videos to post on social media, but video tutorials. These taught an understanding of social media itself in relatable terms that connected entrepreneurs authentically with their customers. Following this, Lucero rethought his business model yet again and launched his highly successful podcast, *The New Generation Entrepreneur.* This success story at last involved full alignment with his authentic self. He had listened to himself, and the universe responded.

Driving Dr. Melissa: Intuition Gets a Lyft

For Dr. Melissa Bird, intuition also kicked off her decision to launch a business and set new priorities and career paths. "In 2017, I was finishing my PhD," she told me. "They expected me to get a job as a professor and a tenure track, but inside I was screaming, *No, that is not what I'm going to do!* Instead, I started my business as a women's business coach" (Bird, 2020).

Dr. Bird listened to her intuition, and it paid off. When she started to lean in even more, her intuition intruded again in the strangest places—like in a Lyft leaving the airport:

> *In the car, I got this random phone call from a friend who said, "I just left a real estate deal to tell you you're supposed to start this company called Natural Born Rebel."*

I always keep a journal with me, and I pulled it out and just started writing this list. The call was fast, but it just called to me intuitively. It was a beautiful, exciting conversation—and the thing that honestly did it was the Lyft driver.

The Lyft driver had heard everything because her phone was on speaker. He turned around, glanced at her, and asked, "Does this stuff happen to you often?"

Her response: "Pretty much."

The best part, though, was his response. "Do you always listen?" Then she said, "Sometimes, but sometimes I don't."

His final comment sealed the deal to creating the book and so much more. "I think you should listen to this one."

By the way, Dr. Bird started writing that book, *Natural Born Rebel*, on the plane home. "I've never had a book flow out of me like that," she says, now four books later.

When you are open to possibilities, you see them when they present themselves to you. You recognize and trust your higher form of consciousness, your inner voice, which you might like to believe is "coincidence," and write it off. Brandon Lucero says:

I don't believe I am just brain and random loose arrows. I think there's a higher soul. I think there's a higher being or consciousness that is really who I am. I think there's a higher version of myself that is depending on me to have these experiences so we can have an evolution of some kind. But I think the more connected you are to that Higher Self, the more you will listen to the Higher Self and the more purpose you will have.

Yet so many times, we find ourselves blocking out our hearts and instincts and letting our minds go into default control. We rationalize; *I can make this work; this person came highly recommended; I can't disappoint so-and-so.* If only I had been aware of and listened to my own intuition, I might have averted a significant business and financial disaster—and certainly have avoided finding myself at the precipice of a life-or-death situation.

Intuition? Time to Listen

My business partner and I were at a conference for venture capitalists involving potential investors at the Four Seasons Hotel at Half Moon Bay, California. I was on stage delivering my presentation pitch on our company to what seemed like a wave of two-hundred-plus men. I also had a 102-degree fever that morning. It took everything I had to stay focused on my intention of manifesting a funder who would invest two million dollars into my startup.

Barely able to walk off the stage, I received a text from a man in the audience. Let's call him Frank. The text said, "I am very interested in investing in your company. I can close out the entire two-million-dollar funding. Can you meet me right now in the lobby?"

My business partner rushed over and said, "You need to go back to the room and lie down."

I showed her the text. "I'm meeting the guy who sent this text." This was 100 percent all Head; I had money to raise. As for my Heart—at that time, *sick* was not in my vocabulary, or that of any rising entrepreneur. Many women in any business, in those days, would not dare to be sick. Sick was a sign of weakness.

My focus was meeting Frank. "You know, I'm very interested," he said. "I love what you're doing. I have tons of resources. We can close out this round of financing for you. And I think this is going to be an absolute unicorn [meaning a rare startup company with a one- billion-dollar valuation—the entrepreneur's impossible dream]." He followed with a strong, "Let's do this."

He added he had a business partner—we'll call him George—who worked on some deals with him, and Frank said I needed to meet this George ASAP. He was from Buffalo, New York, but traveled to the Manhattan area frequently, so we scheduled a meeting the next week.

From the moment I met George, I immediately felt the hair on the back of my neck stand up. I instinctively had a negative feeling about this guy. We got through the meeting, and everything he said was not what my values-driven company was about. And I thought, *I will never do business with this man ... I will not let him in any way have anything to do with this startup.*

When we left, my partner and I laughed at what a complete mismatch he was. But then I got a call from Frank who said, "You know, George thought you were amazing. We want to move forward."

I took a deep breath. "Well, if George is involved, I'm going to have to walk away from the opportunity because I can't work with him."

Frank shot back, "Hilary, why don't we do this? You know we got along really well when we met, and we have joint respect for each other." He ran a billion-dollar fund. "I promise you'll work with me directly. You don't have to work with George at all."

I said, "You know, there was also something I noticed about George. When I pushed him on his background, I found a gap in his business." I never could get to the bottom of that until much later. It turns out George had been involved in an SEC violation that had a penalty that prohibited him from raising any further money for a few years. He was technically at the end of that period when he was trying to get involved with us—and I did like and trust Frank. So, with George out of the picture, Frank and I signed a contract.

Within a month, I got a call. Frank let me know George had connected with a great financial group that was interested in hearing about our company and had the funds and interest to invest.

Again, my instinct to not involve George kicked in.

"Don't worry, you're not going to have to work with him," Frank again assured me. "I will be the point person, and George will just be there to provide backup support and logistics and make introductions." He assured me I would run the meeting.

I needed to keep paying our payroll and keep the development going, so I ended up rationalizing it would only be this one time. *Are you nodding your head right now, saying, "Oh no, don't do it, girl! Yes, in your head it sounds practical, but your heart is saying it feels wrong."* I had an intuition fight right then and there and ignored my own sense of knowing in my Head, my feelings in my Heart, and my good sense in my Higher Self. My intuition lost,

and I ended up making the worst decision of my business career. Have you ever done that? Note: *never do this.*

I closed the door on my intuition, and my head took the lead. I had worked so hard to launch this company that I convinced myself I didn't have a choice.

That week, I flew to New York to meet with George. The meeting went well, and we got eight new investors. The dopamine kicked in, and the thinking became: why wouldn't we work with George? We needed money; he could help us get it. He was past his lockdown period and there were no legal impediments. The gate was opened, and George ended up scheduling a flurry of other meetings and becoming more and more embedded in the fiber of the company. Frank signed an exclusive deal with him because he felt like our success together could absolutely raise the money and create a profitable venture. I was now trapped with the one person I never trusted, and now our company's fate rested in his hands. *What had I done?*

George ended up creating a fund around our company. He set it up so I didn't directly get money from any of the individual investors. They invested in his fund and then George ended up wiring our company the funds indirectly.

It started out looking optimistic for the financial future of the company. Then, gradually, the amounts we received seemed to become significantly less, and the numbers never added up to what I had been told by investors they had been investing. I spoke to George about this repeatedly.

He'd sigh patronizingly. "You understand how people say they're going to do something and then they don't. They end up having other things come up—but we will get there. I'll just need to book more meetings." Chills ran down my body again.

My company never saw the accounting records because George had all the access. So, this cycle of fly around, do a presentation, raise money, and get less money kept going. It became exhausting, and I was never, in his words, "doing enough to keep the business going." It was an ugly situation that, today, you would call emotional abuse—business abuse. I was kept in a perpetual state of spinning, whipping around the country at the last minute, juggling time zones while trying to be a mom to three young kids. George would call on no notice and say, "You need to come tomorrow to XYZ. You have to do these pitches and raise money. If you don't do this, then the shareholders are going to sue you. You know you have a fiduciary responsibility." I always kept a suitcase packed. The choke collar just kept getting tighter.

At one point, I was heading for Africa, and the night before I was leaving, George called and said, "You need to invest more of your own money in this company because when you came out to the East Coast a week ago, you didn't raise enough money. Now we don't have enough to pay the bills and staff and run the company. We're getting close to being able to do this big

deal, but they need to see we have cash to survive six months." He insisted I had to put money in the company right then or we were going to lose it.

My Heart and my Head exploded with anger. I had hit rock bottom. It was like the light went out inside me and I was in a very dark place. At that moment, I felt cornered. *I can't continue to do this. I'm sick all the time. I'm being forced to put money into the company. I'm working nonstop, I'm never around for my kids, and I'm being bullied by the biggest bully I have ever met.* I really would have done anything I could to save the company. I had to come up with a plan and fast. The nagging, horrible feeling inside would not go away, but that message continued to fall on deaf ears. I was too focused on the bottom-line logistics of saving the company to listen.

I ended up investing more money and in one case, ordering a fund transfer literally as I was boarding the plane for Africa. I felt so awful, but I felt trapped between my instincts and a sense of loyalty to what I had built and the shareholders.

Two weeks later, back on the fundraising road, I met George upstate near Buffalo for a meeting. During a two-hour break, he said, "Have you ever seen Niagara Falls?"

When I said I hadn't, he said, "Let's just go by."

Driving up to the Falls, I look out the window and see what looks like clouds of steam as we approach. George parks the car—one in his prized collection—and everything seems to be okay until we get to the path next to the lookout point at the actual Falls.

We are on the American side, and there is a railing, but then the railing ends and you can walk up and look over the river rushing toward Bridal Veil Falls. As I start to walk toward the edge, I hear a crazy voice in my head saying, "Do not get near the edge. Turn around!" This time, I listen, and I follow instructions so quickly I actually run into George, who is standing inches away—uncomfortably, unnecessarily close. I can feel his breath, smell the polish of his smooth, sleek, dark hair, see the tight weave of his navy-blue Brioni suit. He tries to tempt me closer to the railing, asking me questions.

Do I see the rushing water?

Do I see the people down below on the tourist boats?

Do I see the people getting soaked?

My Louboutin stilettos are sliding as I try to navigate the slippery, mist-soaked path. The railing is close, too close for comfort. He has not touched me, but I feel threatened, unsafe. It's like a current is tingling through my body. The Falls generate their own sense of majesty and danger. The tourist site I read online on the drive mentioned in the past hundred years, only ten people have survived falling over the Falls. I'm sure I would not be the eleventh.

Cut!

I envision you now whipping back the cover of this book to check the title. *Wait a minute! Is this a mystery thriller?* Well, it's a thriller, all right, but it's about you—like me—and your thrilling path to your next level of success, which starts with a moment of reckoning, as mine did. It may be a relationship, it may be monetary, it may be your business. Whatever it looks like, it's yours to define. For me, the edge of Niagara Falls was my literal tipping point.

As for the mystery part, sometimes we have to ask ourselves that part of the question too.

1. How did I get myself here?
2. Where do I want to go from here?
3. Why do I feel so lost?

If you find you are asking yourself these questions, you are likely at the edge of something too. I had to ask, when I found myself at the edge of the Falls—and, yes, it's almost too symbolic! How did I, a level-headed businesswoman and entrepreneur, end up feeling I was on the verge of being the ultimate victim—pushed over a railing and swept into Niagara Falls?

Even now, in my mind, I have never been sure if the danger was real or imagined. The only things I know for certain are: 1) I sure as hell didn't want to go over those falls; and 2) I'm here to tell the story—but to me in that moment, that danger was absolutely my reality.

So what is your reality? Science has shown your brain doesn't know the difference—it processes reality and perception as the same thing, then defaults to past experiences for the response (Resnick, 2020). As reported in *Vox* by Brian Resnick, neuroscientist Patrick Cavanaugh points out, "It's really important to understand we're not seeing reality. We're seeing a story that's being created for us" (Resnick, 2020). No wonder we struggle with choices! The final judgment and the ability to choose, to do a ReLaunch Flip, is yours alone. Are you feeling powerful now?

Have you, like me, ever felt helpless or out of control? You probably didn't realize you hold the cards. You are the one who can change and interpret the way you see any situation and impact the outcome you will achieve. That's not helplessness; that's self-control and powerful.

The way our brain works is complex, almost as if we are neurologically constructed to deflect our efforts to make any interceptions. In addition to the fact most of what we believe comes to us preprogrammed from our unconscious minds, other factors stack the deck against us—like that 85 percent of our approximate 6,200 thoughts a day default to negative (Alexander, 2012). If we had to consciously sort through these thousands of thoughts, it would be exhausting. I was an experienced businesswoman, but my mind had defaulted to the script: *George was a person who could help us raise much needed capital. I needed to play the game, go with the flow. Don't rock the boat.*

This is why, in spite of the better judgment, I shook off my instincts with George and found myself standing at the brink of Niagara Falls (in my mind, looking back, I envision Tippi Hedren in an Alfred Hitchcock movie my mom used to watch with me), frozen, ready to either be pushed or rescued—choose one—and I didn't see Cary Grant approaching any time soon to yank me from the brink of disaster.

Then my intuition signaled to me to get out of my head and pay attention to my heart—to recognize in my gut that I had put myself in a precarious position. My Heart and my Head, working together as a team, kicked in and signaled to my Higher Self—*Hilary, it's time to get the hell out of Dodge*. In those nanoseconds, all my 3HQ™ circuits suddenly connected, and my inner engine sparked and ignited with a bang. If there's a hero in this story—in this book—it's the heart. My Heart was my own inner Cary Grant to the rescue. Hearts are like that. They're there to flood your body with feelings; to tell you this is the best puppy to pick from the litter, even though he's the runt; to keep you swiping left or right; to get you off the couch and on that date and perhaps meet the love of your life; to not take a certain job because it didn't feel right; or to stop you from taking candy from the nice man with the van. And, listening to my heart, I lived to tell this tale.

After the Falls incident shook me to the core and the Africa investment demand had left me on high alert, I started the process to ReLaunch the business and open new doors to fundraising. It was time to look at all the possibilities out there, and that day in March 2013, I created a mantra for myself: Launch + Possibility = ReLaunchability. I wanted to take my ability to create abundance and success and ultimately transform, while gaining ground. I raised a million dollars fairly quickly with my new approach. We were really gaining momentum, but at one point, my body rebelled and I got a terrible chest rash—my inner self, via my body, was trying desperately to tell me something again.

I found a substantial investor interested in closing out the last money needed, about two million dollars. Things were very far along and the investment imminent when, suddenly, the investor just dropped out. When I followed up, he said he had begun to question my capabilities. After he had spoken to George, he had questioned the future of the business. I sensed George was angling to take me down with every ounce in my body. Why? He had a reason; I just didn't know it yet.

Soon a power play for a position on my board ensued and things just spiraled from there. I was able to maneuver George off the board, but that only provoked him to take down the company. He threatened a lawsuit, and we ended up in arbitration. The company was over. Things continued to get ugly, and I felt like my heart was broken, but I had one thing going for me: ReLaunchability. I needed to give myself time to mourn the loss of my business and find my way back. It was my time to have a mega-ReLaunch.

Two weeks to the day after the company dissolved, the SEC called me and said they were investigating George. They believed he was siphoning cash from our company and paying off another investment he was involved in. Again, the chills ran up and down my body. My intuition was not saying *I told you so,* but making it present lessons needed to be learned. Finally, it all made sense. The SEC found solid evidence of a Ponzi scheme. I thought back on Niagara and realized if I were out of the picture, nobody would have probably known the depth of his deception. In the end, George was convicted and sent to federal prison for three years.

I later got a surreal letter from him, from prison, written in pencil and full of apologies. He was so sorry, and he suggested we should work together in the future!

By not trusting my own intuition, pushing it down, and not listening to myself, the company shut down, and I possibly almost lost my life. I realize now I was making excuses and interpreting the situation to suit a version of reality I had created. I have since become focused on learning how to trust my intuition and build it into a seriously powerful tool in my 3HQ™ arsenal.

In fact, an article in *Quartz* reports that research has revealed that a majority of leaders use emotions and experience to make decisions, rather than just relying on facts and data (Wilding, 2018). Remember your intuition is the gateway to your Higher Self and best self. It is always with you, and it always has your back. But another pivotal element is involved. You might have to flip your emotions about yourself (Carver and Carver, 2016).

Do I think George would have pushed me over Niagara Falls? All I can advise about that is when you are in a slippery situation, trust your intuition—and leave the six-inch stilettos at home.

QUESTIONS TO THINK ABOUT:

1. Have you ignored your inner voice and missed out on something big?
2. Think back to a time when you had a tipping point. What caused you to find yourself at that moment of reckoning? What changes did you make or actions did you take to move forward from that situation? What were some lessons you learned that help you with future tipping points?
3. The 3HQ™ is a circle, not a line. You can drop into the process at any phase or restart it and begin the loop all over again for a follow-on ReLaunch. Choose a scenario in your life right now; where in the process would you begin to apply the 3HQ™ Method?

PART THREE

HIGHER SELF

CHAPTER EIGHT

FROM SELF-SABOTAGE TO SELF-LOVE

My entire life, I have always been a last-minute type of girl, which somehow led me to also be a Calamity Jayne kind of girl (my middle name is Jayne). I picture myself in college—the one who would always be cramming at the very last minute for a final or test. Then later, with work, I was always making the deadline at the last minute. I might wedge in something like a visit with a friend or some self-created emergency—various reasons to put off focusing on the deadline at hand, putting far more pressure on myself than needed.

I was setting myself up so if something did not come out perfect or with the best grade, I had a built-in default: "Well, this came up last minute ..." I would be able to blame those things instead of feeling like I had "failed." Have you done this? Maybe it's not procrastination, it's perfectionism. Never finishing because of not wanting to fail. Are you seeing your own pattern too?

I had no idea where this was coming from until I got deep into studying neuroscience and understanding the role of past beliefs running automatically to protect me from disappointment. I had to really look into the past to see where this all started. Then it hit me—*first grade!* Failing first grade was a Queen Bee that set the future B.U.G.S. in motion. And that inflated my feeling that I wasn't smart. That image was branded in my mind. No matter how successful I became, it remained deep within me.

Thoughts repeated like a carousal going around and around. If you really put your mind to it and put in a lot of effort—but it doesn't come out the way that you really want? Maybe it's better to do it last minute. Then you always have excuses and reasons why things don't happen exactly as they should have. It's not that you're stupid. Things happen, right?

And when you do have thoughts like those, it's consistently in direct correlation to what you are thinking, since we have our own auto-repeat happening. It's a double whammy; when we think it, the universe delivers it. Like the law of attraction, like attracts like. I was attracting distraction with distraction.

I was the heroine of my own self-created Calamity Jayne show—and perhaps you have your own self-created show title as well.

When the brain sees something that doesn't map to its limiting beliefs and the conditioned thoughts around it, it's like, *Hold it! Wait a second. Let's steer you back to your comfort zone.*

And that's where we hit our wall. That's when we can't move past it. That's sabotage; it keeps getting back to our limiting beliefs that determine how we talk to ourselves. Most of the time, the inner voice is not overly polite and allows you use some choice phrases or words you wouldn't ever say to anyone.

Have you ever felt lacking in some area and created a camouflage plan to cover those perceived deficiencies? What I did was an aggressive defense mechanism plan to offset my deep feelings of not being smart enough. Every time I thought this way, I would take more training and get additional certifications. Then I would see what else I needed. I never had an opportunity to feel like I was not smart enough in that area ... or so I rationalized.

But the B.U.G.S. always eventually surface. I was selected to be a part of a very prestigious speakers' event in Silicon Valley. I had to get my presentation done—so, of course, I kept postponing and putting it off and procrastinating. Finally, it came down to the night before the presentation and I was running out of time.

Can you guess what happened? I got sick and ended up having to wing the entire presentation. When the time came for me to get on stage, I somehow made it through, but I was totally incapable of bringing my best self to an important career milestone. That day, I finally had to accept this was something that had become a deep, self-sabotaging habit for me.

So, as I finally attacked the B.U.G. around this, I realized I don't need to procrastinate, I don't need to be Calamity Hilary Jayne. I realized by giving myself time, I do a lot better. I don't need to build in excuses for what I do. My success is not accidental. By blasting my B.U.G., I gave myself the space and the freedom to give up this protective mechanism I had created.

I finally graduated from first grade.

Work-Life Balance and Other Myths

We've shown examples of the benefits of aligning with the gifts of your inner Higher Self and seen how alignment takes much of the angst off the table. The rewards? More purpose, enjoyment, and happiness (Riggio, 2019). How can balance impact happiness? The implications can be life-altering. Have you been inundated for years with the endless talk of "work-life balance" and spent fruitless and agonizing hours trying—and failing—to hit an impossible mark? In 2013, millions of women bought *Lean In*, the book by Facebook COO Sheryl Sandberg, and the myth of "leaning in" to their jobs, which, a decade later, was

debunked in six studies of two thousand women by Duke University psychologists. Sheryl Sandberg later confessed, "I did not really get how hard it is to succeed at work when you are overwhelmed at home" (Cain, 2018).

In an article that threw more flaming torches onto the popular concept of work-life balance, *Forbes* magazine called this "one of the most harmful myths that has been told in modern society. The concept has been drilled into our heads by so-called experts for years now." Instead, the more meaningful way forward is now purported to be—guess what—in *alignment.* The article "Why Work-Life Alignment, *Not* Balance, is the Key to Happiness" states:

No matter what your work or life situation, we all have twenty-four hours in a day. You get to choose how you spend them. Either live with the tension of a never-ending quest for balance or align yourself and create a life filled with meaning, purpose, and happiness. The effort is about harmony, integration, and alignment to direct all of your energy toward creating a meaningful life (Emaus, 2017).

In her article in *Psychology Today,* "How to Let Go of the Need to Be Perfect," psychotherapist Ilene Strauss Cohen, PhD, comments:

Perfectionism lives and breathes in your fear of making a mistake. When you're afraid of what might happen, you don't always make the best possible choices. Instead, you limit your options because you believe you'll be unable to handle the outcome if it happens to be negative. Allowing perfectionism to run the show is like being on a hamster wheel; you just keep going and going and going, even after you've reached your original goal. You increase the stakes every time, so when you do accomplish something, you wonder if you could have done it better (Cohen, 2018).

Knowing we have roughly 6,250 thoughts a day that float through our minds, if you had to stop and process each and every one of those thoughts independently, the energy it would take would put most people flat (News18, 2020). Your mind, by default, goes into low-power autopilot mode with its number-one job being keeping you safe. It defaults to your pre-fab beliefs while your internal computer ticks along, adding no judgment.

Studies conducted at Stanford University revealed our minds don't see facts or fiction any differently. They process everything as fact. To the mind, "change" is a loaded word (Kolbert, 2017). For instance, while my intuition sensed a threat from George, my mind did not perceive him that way. I unwittingly continued a self-generated cycle of sabotage, which reinforced my own lack of confidence in my decisions. I didn't love or even like myself enough to give my intuition any credibility.

Do you know where you stand in your relationship with yourself? Maybe, like me, you need to commit to learning to like, then love, yourself enough to take on your biggest obstacle—which just might be yourself.

The ancient Chinese general Sun Tzu, that nation's greatest general and military strategist, has been remembered and revered since the fifth century BC for his most famous saying, "Know thy enemy." The full quote goes like this: "Know thy enemy and know yourself; in a hundred battles, you will never be defeated" (Jackson, 2014).

Today, we have the great advantage of science shining a light on the fact that our greatest enemy is often ourselves. So, as I like to think Sun Tzu might have agreed, this is a battle we can't lose.

High Five!

Loving ourselves, which should be the simplest thing in the world, can be a struggle. Clearing the B.U.G.S.—the roadkill of self-acceptance—requires focus, bravery, and time. Therefore, we're leaping—or dragging—ourselves out of bed every morning, facing a new day, the clock ticking, and we look in the bathroom mirror and see the same old us. Maybe you are someone who doesn't look at yourself at all because you already don't like what you see. Imagine not being afraid of a magnifying mirror. The late, great humorist Nora Ephron noted women have it especially tough when it comes to mirrors, inventorying body parts that should make us run in fear if we were able to see them—including, but not limited to, our necks and elbows (Goodreads, 2021). Thanks, Nora. Regardless, we all have our own ways of dumping on ourselves—and lifting ourselves out of the dumps.

But kudos to the woman who has made the mirror our biggest ally. Mel Robbins has had her own successful ReLaunches—from being a lawyer, to a *CNN* analyst, to one of the world's most successful motivational authors, coaches, and the most-booked female speaker in America (MelRobins.com, 2021). She also admits she "spent the first forty years of my life screwing up," until she finally faced down and conquered her inner limitations. Mel figured out how to become her own best friend and fan and give herself the confidence she needed to move forward into the success zone.

Mel says it is so simple, it's almost crazy. "I finally figured out how to change my habits, and I've become a happier, more confident, more fulfilled person because of it."

"If you struggle with self-confidence, making life changes, finding your purpose, or if the general vernacular that encircles self-improvement—words like motivation, inspiration, and passion—leave you more deflated than empowered, I feel you," she says on "Facing Change," episode 360 of *The Rich Roll Podcast.* Her book, *The High 5 Habit: Take Control of Your Life with One Simple Habit,* is about embedding the habit of looking not at, but *in* the mirror every morning and giving yourself a confidence-building High Five—as in, *"No problem! I got this! Great job!"*

Yes, she pulled a flip on the mirror thing. With the wave of a hand, that age-old problematic piece of glass just became our potential best friend forever. The High Five is Mel's version of a small change which, when repeated regularly, will become embedded in your belief system, to the point the habit *becomes* your belief. It's a micro-celebration—of you. After you've done it enough times, the celebration becomes your reality. How long does it take? Mel challenges her followers to try this High Five technique for five days.

The mirror had been Mel's catalyst. Looking in the mirror, she felt she had spent her entire life encouraging other people—her family, friends, her coworkers, and even sports teams—but never herself. She had never, in fact, been excited at the sight of herself in the mirror. In fact, to Mel the mirror was an instrument of self-criticism, a tool she used to pick herself apart.

This simple affirmation, a High Five, gave Mel permission to become her own supporter and cheerleader. It's Mel's belief that taking five seconds out of your day to repeatedly do something encouraging for yourself can actually "change your life" by giving yourself a measure of control that can ultimately lead to a whole lot of changes for the better (Morgan, 2021).

Mel launched a year-long research project about the power of High-Fiving, proving confidence and behavior patterns could be changed by a repetition habit of this simple gesture. In medical environments, work with mirrors and patients attempting to recover movement, such as following an accident, has been shown to impact the neuroplasticity of the brain. This is triggered by small movements—not the same as the High Five, but demonstrating the brain's involvement (Faure, Limballe, and Kerhervé, 2019).

It's likely we are so unconsciously starved for positive reinforcement. Remember, 85 percent of the thoughts we feed through our brains are negative. Signals like the High Five are instant, nontoxic mood elevators. Maybe that's one reason why emojis, smiley faces, fist bumps, and other such positive actions are so popular.

Today, in reaching a state of ReLaunchability, I encourage my clients to stand in front of the mirror every morning and really look into their own eyes, the gateway to the Higher Self, and say:

RELAUNCH MANTRA

I love you, (your name).
Be me, do me, have me back.
I love me (hand gesture).
I love me (hand gesture).
I love me (hand gesture).

HAND GESTURE: +

This ten-second exercise begins the movement from self-sabotage to self-love. Neuroscience confirms that, within as little as three weeks, you can create a new habit (Longman, 2020).

Seemingly insignificant changes—like the High Five or affirmations—move your mind, then your body, into a state of energy, your attitude becomes more optimistic, and your intentions are more likely to be positive.

Researcher, lecturer, author, and corporate consultant Dr. Joe Dispenza has worked extensively in unraveling the mysteries of neuroscience and neuroplasticity. Dr. Dispenza explains a client came to him because she had begun to fall into a deep depression. Every day became more of a struggle, and unable to sleep, she began pondering suicide. Doctors prescribed antidepressants and therapy. He explains:

> *A body can make itself sick by thought alone. So, the problem is now the body is conditioned to the past. And ... once the body is in the mind, the body becomes emotional.*
>
> *You can teach your body to know what the vision of the future is, and then you can turn the battleship around. Put your whole-body biology to reflect what you will feel in the future instead of your past. When your heart is open, you're not in a state of lack. Once the energy starts moving into the heart, it starts to beat in this rhythm, like banging on a drum, or dropping a pebble in the water. Then the heart begins to create a wave of energy, and then all of a sudden, you see this*

wave, and the brain gets its rush of energy. And that can change the brain wave patterns.

This is like the butterfly effect of the brain, when one small action can create a reaction much bigger than itself. A High Five can change your day; a smile can change somebody's life.

Repetition is the mother of learning, father of action, which makes it the architect of accomplishment.

—ZIG ZIGLAR (CHKHETIA, 2019)

QUESTIONS TO THINK ABOUT:

1. Write something down you are afraid will be taken from you. Is this tied to something that happened to you during your childhood? If not, from where did it derive?
2. Have you ever self-created an excuse that became a roadblock stopping you from moving forward toward a goal or in a relationship? Was this a recurring pattern in your life? Make a list of all the times you can recall this has happened and see what they have in common, after you see them on paper.
3. Have you found yourself with self-sabotaging thoughts this week? What situations are you in when these thoughts form? Are these thoughts provable and true? If not, what can you do to quiet these thoughts when you start to think them?

CHAPTER NINE

MANIFESTATIONS, GOOD VIBRATIONS

B.U.G.S. die hard. However, you are in control of your future, dreams, and what you manifest (ReLaunchability). And you can use the Potato Chip Principle to flip away the B.U.G.S. that negatively influence you and replace them with new thoughts and beliefs that will lead to abundance in wealth, relationships, and all areas of life. Here's where you become the writer and director of your own movie. Literally, you can guide your heart and mind to team up in alignment to bring you the career or emotional scenario—even person—of your dreams. Not only have I done this myself, but I have also seen it work over and over. Coincidence? You be the judge after you give it a try.

Manifestation is the process of bringing something you really want into physical reality by focusing on it via meditation, visualization, writing, or tapping into your conscious and unconscious mind. Can you turn an idea into a reality? Scientific evidence shows our beliefs bring about behaviors and responses from others that lead to outcomes we desire. Research shows that our expectations, positive or negative, tend to be confirmed. This is what is known as a self-fulfilling prophecy. Research by Dr. Carol Dweck concludes:

> *It is clearly shown you are more likely to manifest things into reality if you have positive expectations [and] visualize what you desire, it generates positive emotions.*
>
> *[On the other hand,] if you don't think you can succeed in some goal, let's say getting your dream job, you'll set in motion events that will actually make it more likely you won't get your dream job. Repercussions such as being in a bad mood, late for the interview, or just projecting a negative attitude can all play roles in this less-than-desirable outcome (Davis, 2020).*

As Jim Fortin points out:

> *I think some people think they're supposed to just stand there and wave the magic wand and go "Shazam!" and the money is supposed to show up. It doesn't happen that way because the external world reflects your internal world. And if your internal world is poor and has no money, then you repel money. You can learn how to use emotion and frequency to attract what you want.*

This is where vibrations come in. Everything—tangible or intangible, objects, feelings, people, emotions, even entities like companies—is said to have a frequency of its own, based on a level of energy that it gives off or vibrates (Wong, 2021). If you train and use your feelings and emotions to identify the vibrations of what it is *you* desire, you are more likely to attract like-minded entities.

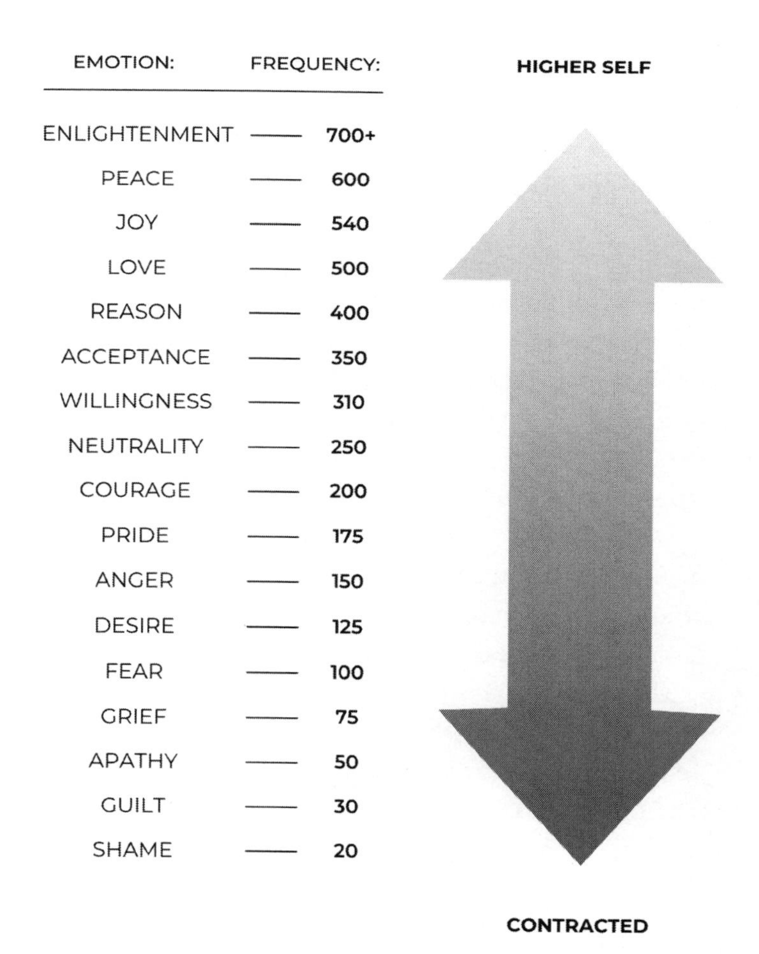

The Barometer of Balance

For instance, love has a vibration level on the Emotional Vibration Chart of 500 hertz, and joy is at 540 hertz. Fear, by the way, is at one hundred hertz, with shame and blame at thirty to forty, so when you can become aware of what you are feeling and know the vibration score, you can then realize you need to be at that level or above to bring in similar like-energy things into your life. And this is leveraging the law of attraction that *like attracts like.*

You can raise your own vibration until it aligns to match. You can manifest the object of your desire, like the love of a great job or relationship.

Your level of vibration will attract things, people, situations, experiences, and outcomes with the same vibration. Think of it this way: our emotions are energy, which have vibration, and like attracts like. It makes you powerful to be able to decide what thoughts you are going to think so your emotion is at a higher level, making you a ReLaunchability powerhouse.

When we operate at a lower level of energy, our vibration is low, and our emotions follow—we might feel like a victim, for example. We blame others, or circumstances, for not achieving what we desire. The power of the 3HQ™ expands positive energy, which is far more likely to attract positive outcomes, like the instant and magnetic attraction of a couple that is "made for each other" or a job interview that checks all the boxes.

SUCCESS MANIFESTATION MAGNET

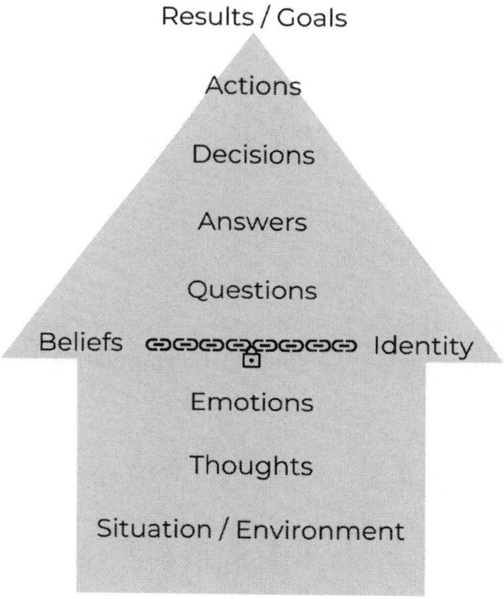

Results / Goals

Actions

Decisions

Answers

Questions

Beliefs Identity

Emotions

Thoughts

Situation / Environment

The point is to achieve focus and clarity so your mind can really allow that like-minded energy into your life. Science endorses this as increasing the chances of success. According to *Psychology Today*, mental practices (like visualization) can boost motivation, confidence, and even motor performance. In fact, researchers found that for athletes, guided visualization resulted in feeling the positive emotions of winning the game or healing their body and may increase energy levels and "give a boost" in winning competitions (Goldsmith, 2013). Basically, you have a built-in internal cheering section that is yelling out, "*Go, us!*"

Yet you can create that rocket-fueled boost through external, and internal, ways. Several studies from Oxford found vision boards can also help make goals a reality (Becker, 2021).

Your method may range from writing in a journal (my recommendation, due to the 3HQ™ direct physical connection through the hand that is writing to the mind and heart), mindful meditation, repeating or writing an affirmation, saying the ReLaunch Morning Mantra, or just talking to a friend to spark the connection vibration.

BElieve-It Boards: Your Go-To Magic

Have you heard the phrase "seeing is believing"? A vision board engages the mind and attracts a focal point for energy around whatever it is that you desire. Not all psychologists agree about the effectiveness of vision boards in the manifestation process, but most agree that a board can help direct you to achieve short-term goals activated in the here and now. That's a powerful "first step" (Morin, 2018).

My version of a vision board takes it a step further into what I call a BElieve-It Board. It is a key secret to creating successful outcomes with your manifestations. Ask yourself, *Who do I need to be to achieve my goals?* To make it all happen, you must be that person—from your thoughts to your emotions, to your beliefs, to the questions you ask, to the decisions you make, and to the actions you take. Without this alignment step, your dream board/vision board is incomplete.

Not only do these boards help you focus on and maintain specific goals, but they allow you to find clarity on what you want and how you're going to get there. Similar to vision boards, BElieve-It Boards serve as motivation to reach your goals. However, unlike most vision boards, BElieve-It Boards will keep your focus on your "why" and tie that inspiration and motivation to the emotions and feelings behind each image. This serves as a visual reminder to be who you need to be and to do what you need to do in order to have the life/career/relationships you've always wanted.

You can cultivate inspiration in so many ways, and to me, they're all fun. You can create your board however you wish. Tear out pictures from magazines, clip quotations, add details from nature (shells for a beach wish or dried leaves, herbs, and flowers for a nature vision), write an actual check

with a dollar amount for money, or paint your own picture or write in your own words. You don't need to be an artist; it's just a representation. The important thing is your board represents your inner picture of what you want. There are no set rules, and what you wish to manifest may be a big thing or something smaller. The key is not what it is, but your ability to hone in and focus on it.

When I create my BElieve-It Board, I see the end result of what I want to manifest in my mind. Legendary personal development trainer Zig Ziglar coined the phrase, "Be, do, have." The principle is that, in order to attain the most meaningful things in life, you first have to "*be*" the right kind of person, then you must "*do*" the right things so you can "*have*" these things. BEing the person who would get the outcome, DOing the actions that would create momentum, and then HAVE what you want to occur (New Paradigm

Advisors, 2021). Adding these concepts into the board with words, images, and objects representing emotions increases the results-oriented power of the exercise because you incorporate your identity into the manifestation process of what is to come. You are now taking your BElieve-It Board from the Head to your Heart, to your Higher Self, leveraging the full potential of the 3HQ™ in creating your best outcome. That's what I try to reflect in my own boards, which are extremely detailed and focused, as have been my outcomes.

BElieve-It or Not

My husband? Believe it or not, he came to me on a BElieve-It Board. After one divorce and breaking up with a nonstarter guy eleven times, I was ready to bring a man into my life who would be a keeper. I finally realized I was ready for a truly meaningful relationship. I wanted a soulmate. I wanted to be able to do things like enjoy food, travel, hike, have meaningful conversations, and be passionate about life and each other, so this board was going to need to be a level above anything I had created before. It was hyper-focused specifically on that desired relationship.

I divided the board into quadrants. The first was the quadrant around what we would do as a couple. Then another quadrant was around what he would look like when we were together doing the things we loved. Optimistically, I even included a quadrant of how he was going to ask me to marry him (including, insanely optimistically, a picture of my future engagement ring).

Another quadrant was on the emotional side of how I would feel. In the middle of the board, I put who I needed to be in order to attract the energy of a man like the one I was creating. I knew she would be confident, vulnerable, self-aware, adventurous, and intriguing. I started to act with those characteristics in my daily life.

I wanted to be ultra-clear about everything, so I then created a movie in my mind that took in every single one of the areas of the board I created. I started to add the emotional side, how it would feel to be around this man. I brought my future to life on my BElieve-It Board with an unwavering sense it would happen.

And what happened? After being set up, I walked into a bar, this man stood up, and I recognized him instantly. *Oh my god, that's him. That's the guy on my BElieve-It Board.* It really was like the movie I'd made in my mind, flying sparks and all. He was there, and I was ready. Quantum physics were merging my future with my present reality right in front of me. It was like two planets colliding. Incredibly, he looked exactly like a slightly older version of the guy from my BElieve-It Board.

His name was Erich, and after dating a couple of months, I showed him my BElieve-It Board (I might have put a Post-it temporarily over the picture of the ring). He was a little blown away at the board, while I was still in disbelief he was single and available at the exact time I was looking.

I was curious about his journey to meeting me:

> *Well, I've been single for almost seven years and I said to myself in March, "I am now ready to meet somebody seriously in my life. I'm not focused on casual dating.*

> *I'm now focused on bringing in and manifesting the one woman for my life."*

He was ready and clear about what he was looking for, so he put it out there and, as he has said, "the universe delivered."

My Head had to retrain the way I thought and reset the neuro pathways of what was possible. To open up to not just a new relationship, but to attract love, set up my heart for a new way of *having* a relationship, and operate from my Higher Self and emanate an energy vibration of love. The 3HQ™ Effect is a fluid process. What goal, outcome, or priorities have not manifested for you? What change do you want? Once you have taken one of your limiting beliefs through the Belief Blaster™, you have a map to leverage the process to create new positive habits and empowering beliefs. The key point is readiness. Nothing can really happen until you have cleared out your B.U.G.S. Then the momentum begins.

Once you have identified the emotional block in your heart and removed it, your core values and your new beliefs are freed to become aligned with your new identity. Now you've achieved the balance necessary for the peak performance your 3HQ™ is capable of delivering.

The next step is maintaining that balance so you can hold onto those gifts you've brought into your life. Manifestation and mindset coach Lea Fuentes recommends reassessing your manifestation practice monthly, while keeping on the lookout for signs that your work is taking root. "If something seems like a positive coincidence, don't brush it off," she says. "Take it as a sign, because it almost always is!" (Buzzell, 2021).

I still have the BElieve-It Board I created that brought Erich into my life. I still think *wow*

when I look at the experiences on that board, the emotions I included, and even the actual

ring he put on my finger.

I chose a relationship goal. What will you choose? Now, it's *your* time.

Okay, you're saying. *You met a great guy. He had the right look—and the right ring. But ...*

I admit a BElieve-It Board is not quantitative science, and Isaac Newton probably didn't use one (maybe Leonardo did ...). Yet as I am writing this, I got an affirming call from someone who is not only a client, but a dear friend, with a story that is yet another example of how all this works together.

Shona Gupta is an amazing woman in tech and an innovative entrepreneur. Based in Los Angeles, Shona has decades of experience in technology and brand and business development that is backed up by her MBA. Born in India and raised and educated in Canada, she spent two years teaching in an Indian village, where she forged and strengthened her cultural connection to her family's heritage and formed a commitment to education for girls. That bond stuck with her for life and, following an executive career in the corporate world, Shona felt an inner shift in her values. The question was how could she fulfill this while still maintaining the steady job her family responsibilities required?

Transition and transformation in a career are usually not instantaneous, like an on/off light switch; the process is more like sliding the dimmer and slowly illuminating the space that is your life. What you want evolves within that inner "gallery space." On a call with me, Shona shared her determination to make a positive impact and her parallel passion to redefine her gallery space.

Shona's full-time job was super demanding. She spent most of her negligible spare time concocting business strategies while mom duty kept her calendar packed. But in the little cracks in her day, she decided to try using the steps we discussed leading up to the BElieve-It Board.

Leveraging her business acumen and studying the market, Shona detected a gap in the skincare segment: there was nothing on the Western luxury market for women like her with brown skin and specific skincare and beauty biochemistry. Shona decided to merge two powerful modalities of Indian skincare—plant-based beauty and CBD science—together. With her employer's blessing (and investment), Shona developed a unique skincare line integrating CBD with Ayurvedic and ancient Indian beauty ingredients, including secrets passed down from her grandmother and extended family. The result was Maharindee, a buzzworthy brand of all-natural, organic, vegan skincare products. Shona was determined to manifest the new dream day job that would allow her to take her ambitious side gig to the next level.

Figuring she had nothing to lose, Shona started envisioning her BElieve-It Board imagery as soon as we hung up. In just a few weeks, she got a call and the new job she had manifested was offered to her.

She now had her job, her product, and her brand, but she still needed extra funding that would allow her to get it into the marketplace. She focused on manifesting her end goal and put up a crowd-funding site. After quickly overshooting her initial goal, she was thrilled when yet another funding source kicked in. Manifestation or market savvy? Probably a lot of both.

The Cultural Component

Shona's early experiences teaching in the Indian village play a role as well, and Maharindee pays it forward. "We donate a percentage of all profits to a terrific program called Room to Read, which enables girls to stay in school throughout countries like Asia, India, and Africa."

Cultural empowerment and the emergence of female-founded brands brought Shona back emotionally and full circle to her powerful, inspirational female heritage. Research has shown neural function and perception are indeed impacted by culture, but it's only recently that this fact has become monetized in the development of new products and brands like Maharindee (Park and Huang, 2010; "How the Inclusive Beauty Movement," 2021).

Shona's brand is an example of how 3HQ™-driven offerings bring a new kind of dynamic energy and community-driven platform that elevate business and cultural values, expanding into new aspects of opportunity. On *The* ReLaunch *Podcast*, we discussed how a concept taken out of the Head ("skin care and beauty") and into the Heart (traditional Indian ingredients with the legacy of Shona's grandmother) aligns with the 3HQ™.

Culture is infinitely complex, but family values is a concept most of us can share. As Dr. Brenda Wade—a noted psychologist, entrepreneur, transformation coach, and past chair of the San Francisco Human Rights Commission—notes, "We are all human beings, children of Mother Earth."

This is an opportunity for not just a product, but also unity and coming together with like energy.

Family values in the company value proposition? My mom, for one, would certainly approve.

Questions to think about:

1. Like attracts like. Your level of vibration will attract things, people, situations, experiences, and outcomes with the same vibration into your life. When we operate at a lower level of energy, our vibration is low and our emotions follow. What thoughts are you going to think to raise your level of vibration to manifest what you desire?
2. What core values enhance and raise your level of vibration to manifest what you desire?
3. Create your BElieve-It Board. What images, sayings, or objects will you put on your BElieve-It Board? If these were to become your reality, how would that make you feel and how would it change your life?

CHAPTER TEN

READY, SET, RELAUNCH

One day, looking at my schedule, I realized I spent more time putting together my to-do list than examining, or even thinking about, my inner needs. Meanwhile, I was a total workaholic-slash-wanna-be-Supermom, leaping on planes in a single bound, pounding out PowerPoints with fingernails of steel, helping with homework long distance, and catching the leak under the sink with x-ray vision all while fighting the realities of endless fundraising and exhaustion while running on depleted adrenalin. Failure—or what I perceived as failure—at anything was not an option! Meanwhile, something deep inside was yelling itself hoarse: *Hilary, what's wrong with this picture?*

I had so much to be grateful for. In some ways, it didn't make sense. In others, I could spot it a mile away, and it made all the sense in the world; it's our blind spot. I now can look back and say recognizing the blind spot is key to getting a perspective on B.U.G.S. In my case, my workaholic queen B.U.G. had shot off so many tentacles she pervaded my entire life, like a forest of runaway weed vines choking off the garden. Putting on makeup in the car while driving the kids to school? *Check.* Doing homework with them via phone from New York? *Check.* Marriage circling the drain? *Check.* That's where self-realization and self- coaching come to a crossroads.

My key to self-realization—to the awareness something was out of alignment—came from stepping outside my comfort zone, in the unlikely form of a TV reality show. For you, it might be a family event, a situation at work, or a blowup where you just can't take it anymore.

Having my own business and becoming a successful entrepreneur who could make a difference had long been one of my goals. As I maneuvered into the core of California's cutting-edge entrepreneurial community, one would say I'd been successful—on the outside—and on a quest to find and fund the business that was going to change the world. On the inside, however, I was not the confident woman I appeared to be. I felt I was just a very good actress, participating in a charade. The impostor syndrome was still clinging to me. But by this time, I'd Houdini'd myself into conjuring up a pretty good show, with a wall of accolades. What I didn't realize was that was part of the problem. Whirling faster and faster, checking off more awards and successes, was not making me feel better about myself. The ticking time bomb was set.

Helping others wherever I could had always been at my core, personally and in business, so when I was asked to be on *ABC's The Secret Millionaire* reality TV show, the fuse was lit. I felt it was a great chance to make a bigger impact. The show had an entirely worthy goal: to help others and give nonprofit organizations and their incredible work a voice, visibility, and a monetary contribution, which would provide much-needed financial support as well as awareness of their amazing work. However, as it ended up, it was *I* who was helped by them. This was where I had a big lightning bolt of self-realization—and the beginning of yet another life-altering transformation.

As Dr. Wade explains, "Most people stick to the paths that have been encoded in their brains." And then we wonder why the outcomes don't change or improve and why we don't feel any better about ourselves (why, for instance, five awards didn't make me feel any better than one). After all, you've invested so much of yourself into this path. Change is risky. Maybe things would be worse if you veered off course, and we know our subconscious likes certainty and despises change.

Yet that very fact of repeating the same patterns also results in a lack of opportunities to grow, evolve, or change. It's also easier to look at other people, your job, or your situation, and put the blame there—it's them, not you, right? The cement for these attitudes has hardwired our brains and left little room for our hearts, which are struggling to be heard. Being off-balance internally, even when we are well-off superficially, causes a lack of personal alignment that makes us intuitively realize something is not right. So how do we handle that? We jump right back onto the hamster wheel ASAP to "fix" it. Exhausting, right? Not to mention adrenal fatigue, burnout, or even a total identity/midlife crisis.

When and how do we put on the brakes and say, "Stop. I really do need to fix this. I need to fix myself. I can't go on like this anymore"? This is a signal you are ready to evolve. The discomfort factor, and the feeling of being out of alignment, will force us to become aware. Take note of this; it could be your tipping point.

At the critical milestone of our mid-zone, we enter a new phase of growth, much as we once did as babies or young children (Kunst, 2011). Many times, when we are feeling the most dissatisfied, unhappy, or unworthy, it's because where we thought we should be at this stage of life does not match up with our own reality. This leaves us feeling like failures. The key is to listen to ourselves and recognize the tipping point when it happens. And we will sense it, because the discomfort factor, the feeling of being out of alignment, will force us to become aware. For me, *The Secret Millionaire* TV show set off this kind of discomfort. My environment suddenly shifted, and it was like the kaleidoscope made a turn and all the images realigned.

The Secret Millionaire

During shooting, the producers avoided the Hollywood treatment to keep the focus on the charities and those they were serving. They set me up in a small house in one of the worst areas of Long Beach, California. "Wardrobe" was simple, non-frills, and no fuss. The point was to blend in, not stand out. My house was filthy, so I spent my first night Clorox-ing, Lysol-ing, and cleaning. It was not uncommon to discover rat droppings in the morning. I found out from a neighbor somebody had been shot on the corner the week before. What had I signed up for? I thought of my kids, my own clean house. After that first night, I called the show producer and told her I didn't think I was a good fit. Maybe

I was the wrong person for this job. Maybe reality TV was a bit too real for me. Or maybe this was exactly why I needed to be there.

Regardless, the producers gave me no out. They had an objective, which was trying to break me down by giving me only minimum wage for food purchases and removing anything that reminded me of home. Finding gratitude is about minimalism, stripping things out to the essence so the precious gems can be appreciated. Well, on this show, they were ripping everything out so I could show up in a better place and meet individuals on a more loving and empathetic level. That's when the real connection happened.

I knew I couldn't leave. I needed to learn and share a much bigger lesson. I realized this was a microcosm with no real comparison to the hardships and lifestyle of the people this show was trying to help, but it was still a real eye-opener. It planted a seed that would continue to grow long after the show was over.

During shooting, I got involved in everyday tasks, down to shoveling horse poop for a charity that offered equine therapy, meeting the homeless and giving them sandwiches, and creating a memorial for a young boy who had died. Looking back, the fact I was thought of as a "secret millionaire" makes me cringe. For many of the problems and situations I saw, money helped, yet it was not the ultimate solution. How do you replace a child? How do you keep helping others when you can barely pay your own bills? How do you feed others when no donations were coming in? These are heart-wrenching questions.

The things I saw on this show and the people I met really opened my eyes. Granted, it was only a week and it was only a TV show—a tiny, curated slice of real life—and so trivial compared to so many other major issues. But the situations and the people and emotions involved were real—more real, as it turned out, than my life. That show forced me to turn inward and look deeply at the identity I had created for myself for the first time in a long time—maybe ever. It awakened something inside me. The cement foundation that had held my brain captive for so long finally began to crack.

I'd been living almost entirely in my Head—running a business, seeking investors, managing my family's schedule, traveling, speaking, presenting, having calls, meetings—step after step. I had no room left for my Heart. On the show, however, I was forced out of my Head and into

my Heart, forced to see a glimpse of a world from which I was so far removed. It finally jolted me into seeking some kind of perspective on my own life.

Many of the volunteers were struggling to even make ends meet. Nonetheless, they were dedicating their lives to helping others. It was incredible. That's when I said to myself, *Hilary, what are you doing? You think you're a philanthropist because you're writing checks, but you don't know anything about who you're donating to. You don't know anything about this kind of struggle.*

At the time of the show's filming, I was running a company dedicated to trying to keep kids safe online, a noble cause even today. But working side by side with an eight-year-old who was providing stuffed animals to homeless children, watching a woman give so much of herself to people who had experienced such loss, and working into the late hours of the night so another child could be comforted by a horse and avoid going back to an unfit home were life-changing experiences. I had no indication, going into the show, that was where it was going to end up.

That person who had been shot right on the corner by the house where I was staying? A kid was left without a parent. And it was a wake-up call. *This is life. This is what it's all about.*

I started to think about what I would do in my work, while also asking myself what I was really doing in my personal life. At first it felt odd, but I was driven to express in writing what I felt for the first time in years. I wrote and wrote in my journal. The words flowed, and you know what? I started to connect with myself, to bring my invisible self to the visible surface on those pages. I started to question everything, spending my nights asking questions like:

- *What did I really want?*
- *Who did I really want to surround myself with?*
- *What was my legacy?*
- *How did I want to show up for my kids and family?*
- *What limiting beliefs were holding me back?*

I found myself far outside my comfort zone, in situations that allowed me to see that who I had become was not in alignment with who I wanted to be. Coming into the show, I thought I was checking all the boxes. I thought, as a single mom, that I was proud of my "juggling" capabilities. In the space of that week, however, I was meeting single moms living *on the street* with their kids, people who would have thought the disgusting house I was in for one measly week was an unaffordable luxury. Issues started flooding to the surface. I realized I had been wrestling with a few very big B.U.G.S. of my own.

Sue Beeney, who represented one of the charities, was an expert in grief counseling. From many years of experience, this woman was almost psychic. She had such an ability to hone in

on the crux of things. Sue was there to help the families, but as we discussed the situation, she suddenly asked me, "Have you ever lost anybody?"

An image flashed: *My mom is walking into my room with the saddest expression on her face. I'm twelve, doing homework at my desk. She tells me she has some sad news. "Your grandparents were driving back from an event in San Francisco, and your grandfather had a heart attack while he was driving. There was a terrible car accident."*

Sue asked me how I handled it, how we handled it as a family. I said, "I can't really remember." She pulled out of me the fact I still didn't have closure. My parents had divorced, we never had a memorial, and we just moved on. Nobody really discussed it, even though our hearts were broken; we just put it behind a door in order to move on. So, from a Heart perspective, I never mourned. And from then on, I just opened and closed another door when things got too tough. This became my ingrained behavior, my default mechanism, and part of my belief and operating system.

Sue asked me, "So when do you plan on actually mourning your loss?" At that point, I just broke down right there on the show, and she gave me a big hug—one of many.

That's when I realized my limiting belief, the ingrained behavior standing in the way of evolving, was: *be strong; you don't let emotions get in the way of what you're trying to do.* I had been so busy playing the role of the supermom executive. My Head had been blocking the emotions in my Heart for so long—but that's not actually strength. In reality, it holds you back.

Burying my feelings deep inside created a barrier to my true emotions, heart, and self that this experience on the show started to break down. I had to wonder—what had the impact been on so many aspects of my life, my core relationships, and my work?

By no coincidence, I always felt unsettled. I did know one thing for sure: this wasn't just about me. If I did not want my children to grow up with the same limitations, to have free choices and not behavior predetermined by patterns I had set for them in their early lives, I had to educate myself and understand how this all worked. But as I got to know the wonderful people on the show and these gut-wrenching scenarios they dealt with every day, my thinking changed concerning which beliefs I wanted to continue to live by and which were ready to be released so I could transform into my new aspirational identity.

As I awarded the checks to the charities in the unveiling ceremony, I got chills up and down my body. I remember thinking, *I'm not who I was when I came into this.* I made a promise to myself to make it stick. *I'm not going to lose what just happened to me. I'm not going to let that disappear.* To this day, I focus on leaning into my Heart—feeling and being true to my own inner calling, and helping others find theirs.

Neuropsychologist Dr. Shannon Irvine gave me valuable advice based on her experience when deciding to make a shift and expand her business:

> *I wanted my kids to grow up in a world where they know they have the tools to get whatever they want. And that can't happen unless enough people get the training to help other people with it. Then the educators get that training, and they understand how the brain works. I became obsessed with brain science and finding out how people hear your message.*

I was one of those who heard her message loud and clear.

Up, Periscope

Before the show, I was full of guilt that my company was faltering. I had allowed spreadsheets and self-doubt to stand in the way of trusting my instincts, my inner voice, my intuition. But now I had cleared out a throughway to think with my heart and access the higher feelings behind my decision-making. By leveraging my 3HQ™ and accessing a higher level of self, I was able to unify my mixed messages and say, "You know what, I'm going to do this, and trying and failing is far better than sitting on the sidelines." Critically, I was able to look toward what was next as not leaving behind a failure, but as an amazing opportunity, instead of seeing what I would leave behind as black marks that hindered me. I flipped the script and gave myself permission to be grateful for what had come before and to love the people in my life for how they added to my journey. I looked ahead, and it was as if the prescription on my glasses had changed. A vision of myself as a powerhouse of possibility unfolded before my eyes. That moment, when I saw and embraced the flip of the script, was when my transformation really began.

"Stella," as I'll call her, is the CEO of a pioneering healthcare data company, which she led from founding to a valuation of $500 million. In spite of her success, she remains uncomfortable, unsure of her next steps, and haunted by B.U.G.S. that she traces to her earliest years as a helpless daughter watching her dad struggle in his business.

> *I think back, and my dad had a few businesses. He wasn't successful in any, but he was very intelligent and knew exactly what customers needed. I don't know why he wasn't successful; however, I feel watching how he failed at business has somehow handcuffed me to the fear I can't make it happen. That's my biggest B.U.G.—my "Queen Bee"—and I had to overcome it to be successful. On the opposite end of the spectrum, I can see my business is successful. Between now and the end of that spectrum is this huge void/gap I can't seem to get across. It's like I'm trapped in the middle of a long bridge. Should I go forward, stay where I am, or turn back?*

I'm lost and feeling confused with no certain way to turn. At my age, I should have it all together knowing where I'm coming from, where I am, and where I'm going. Mentally, my character is beaten up by this constant thought to the point it's almost suffocating, and my thoughts lead to wanting to just throw in the towel. On the other hand, my will to go on is strong, because I've been told so often during my childhood we're not quitters, and we come from a strong bloodline—so I don't quit. It's exhausting just having to relive my childhood. I think about it entirely too much, to the point where I hesitate or do nothing at all. Time wastes away and so do missed opportunities, and I don't know it until it's too late.

I asked Stella if she thought the stranglehold her past beliefs had on her was sabotaging her chances for greater successes. When things are not moving forward as they should, you may feel it in your back, your neck, or your gut. This is an indicator, telling you there's some kind of resistance. When things are working, when you're in the groove, you have alignment and you're moving forward. However, when things are not, you get resistance and struggle. I challenged Stella's awareness of her B.U.G.S. and that she could go in a completely different, empowering direction by transferring them to a secure, self-aware space where she could open a dialogue with herself, blast her B.U.G.S. to oblivion, and open up opportunity. We all have the ability to activate our Belief Blaster™. Stella is a great example of generational beliefs not having to continue. You can flip the story and put it to work for the future of yourself and your family.

It's important to keep in mind your personal ReLaunch is customizable; it can take many forms. The 3HQ™ ReLaunch is not just about corner offices, bonuses, promotions, or mastering the best relationships. It's about your new mindset and starting on the path to loving yourself, being aware, and making conscious, mindful choices—being open to being *you.* Maybe, as I was, you are that "scattered entrepreneur," facing that mid-zone tipping point of your life and career, or, like Stella, asking yourself what to do next and hitting inertia.

Ask yourself if you are ready to take action toward your future goals. Are you ready to elevate what you are already doing, as I am now trying to do, right here, right now, writing this book? In the course of our lives, we may have numerous tipping points where we are ready for a ReLaunch. Some are smaller, some wider in scope; all are, in some way, life changing. *Ready, set,* ReLaunch can be a motto for a lifestyle of upward transformation. It's a circle, each transformation leading us back to our Higher Selves, which keeps rewarding us with the validation that we are the individuals we have always had the potential to be.

QUESTIONS TO THINK ABOUT:

1. Do you feel aligned in your work/life right now? If so, or if not, why? What could you do differently, starting now, to become more aligned in your lifestyle?
2. Do you feel you send yourself mixed messages? Do you become aware of how this can throw you out of alignment with your 3HQ™?
3. What can you do to become a bigger advocate for yourself?

CHAPTER ELEVEN

JOURNEYING TO YOUR UNIQUE PURPOSE

Until I blasted some B.U.G.S. of my own, it seemed like I was being held back by an invisible force. I'd been thinking about new ways to get the ReLaunch message to more people. Doing a podcast had been a dream for over two years, but I always seemed to find an excuse for why now wasn't a "good time." I would somehow encounter another setback, another transition, another fill-in-the-blank. It remained on my "SomeDay" list—a day that never came. Pause here for a moment. Maybe get a cup of coffee or tea after you read the next sentence and see what comes to mind: what's on your "SomeDay" list that you keep pushing off? Maybe that should be your priority.

In my case, it was my body—in its usual response—that intervened. It needed to shut down for me to force myself to figure out my priorities. I lost my voice for five days during the pandemic—the thirty-ninth case in San Francisco. Due to this health crisis, I was forced to stop the chatter in my head and focus on myself. It turned out the person in there might have been shy, but she was mighty when she finally roared.

What are you doing? My inner voice yelled at me, as if uncaged. *Who are you?* My personal "SomeDay" goal of starting a podcast was suddenly upon me. I knew it was possible this transition in my business model could also trigger the more holistic personal transformation I had dreamed of for so long.

I got out of my Head—and what I now call the "SomeDay Syndrome."

I got into my Heart; instead of focusing on the logistics of the studio setup, the equipment, and the schedule, I flipped my thinking and focused on the communication aspect, the Heart of it all, and thought about audio as a way to have an emotional connection to more people. This was a more intimate, immediate way to help the audience connect to their greater selves. A new conversation had begun, and the idea took off from there. Once I got out of my Head and into my Heart, it was so liberating and fulfilling.

For me, ReLaunch that has fueled growth has been a lifelong, circular process. In late March 2020, I launched *The* ReLaunch *Podcast.*

You'll find, as you move out of the vice grip of the beliefs stuck in your head and into the emotion of your heart, that your energy levels vibrate at a different, higher level. That's when you begin to attract like-minded, positive energy emanating from elements more aligned with your new goals. On low energy, you can only attract similarly like-minded low energy. Now, however, you can pull in more fuel for your fire. The fireflies of your spirit and energy burn more brightly. The gratitude you feel for this more enlightened, energized state—and the opportunities you now can acknowledge—lifts your energy vibration level further still and boosts you to your Higher Self. This elevation makes you feel powerful and purposeful since you are tapping into the positive real estate of love and joy.

Discovering Your Unique Purpose

Our subconscious wears a blindfold. It doesn't know the difference between a good belief versus a bad belief, a good habit and a bad one (Duke, 2018). We find ourselves in neutral, unable to change our identity from that person who always reacted in a certain way because the beliefs that identity was built upon are still unchanged. This could mean, for instance, you want to get a new job, or any job, or move your business's bottom line up from six figures to seven or eight. Meanwhile, deep in the quicksand, your mind is still self-identifying as the person with no job, or the person who's been in the same job forever, or the six-figure bottom-liner. But hey, no judgment because the truth does set you free, and we are on a quest of freedom.

But when the tipping point pushes you over the edge and you feel it's time to invest in *you*, you will dare to start thinking about investing in yourself in new ways. No matter what you're facing, appreciate that insight and take responsibility.

One step then leads to another until you have a path forward, and the magic is uncovered.

Science has discovered it's our purpose that helps set us apart as individuals, unique from other people, while also setting us up to better function as a group, a team, or a society. A meaningful purpose acts as a kind of nourishment for the soul. Developing meaningful, purposeful goals are associated with developing both physical and mental health (Smith, 2018).

How do successful people discover and apply their unique talents to live their unique purpose? They do it their way. Entrepreneur Kara Goldin, founder and CEO of Hint, a line of naturally fruit-flavored waters, redefined success on her terms when she decided she wanted to live a life with more purpose but didn't know exactly how to get there. She did know she wanted to be healthy, spend more time with her kids, and find a career she was passionate about.

"Sometimes, it takes a very small thing to present you with a wake-up call," she explained on *The* ReLaunch *Podcast.* For Kara, this involved a can of soda. She realized she was drinking twelve sodas a day at work and that this was not only unhealthy but also made her a bad role model for her family.

After swapping what she calls her "Diet Coke addiction" for plain water, she saw improvements in her energy level, complexion, and weight. But she wasn't very excited about taking a "water break." That's when the light went on (Downes, 2020).

In 2005, Kara took matters into her own hands and started experimenting with homemade kitchen concoctions of different non-sugar fruit flavors (Fortune Editors, 2021; Georgiadis, 2021).

The seemingly small lifestyle change Kara made at the beginning of her ReLaunch journey—avoiding sodas and flavored water—eventually led her to reach her goals and push herself far past all her expectations.

How does a waitress with no beverage experience leap to become one of Fortune 500's most admired CEOs? Kara learned by doing. Today, at California Polytechnic State University (Cal Poly in San Luis Obispo) where I'm fortunate to sit on the Foundation Board, I see the 3HQ™ process at work in the Learn by Doing approach. Students are being taught to go beyond what is simply said. They're taught to challenge and test by doing. This leads them from the textbook/laptop and the Head to their emotions in their Hearts—and a sense of purpose emerges. As President Jeffrey Armstrong says, "At Cal Poly, Learn by Doing is a deliberate process whereby students, from day one, acquire knowledge and skills through active engagement and self-reflection inside the classroom and beyond it" ("Learn by Doing," 2021). Why not take the Learn by Doing approach in your own life and work toward creating your own sense of purpose—and beyond?

For example, looking back on her story as an inspiring author and spiritual leader, Kim Woods seemingly had it all: a successful career as an IT consultant, a loving husband, and wonderful children. Her life should have been perfect—there's that word, "should"—yet it wasn't. A dissatisfaction brewed inside of her. She knew she could find more to her life and story somewhere out there. This led her on a powerful journey to find who she was meant to be, taking her from corporate consultant to spiritual leader. Kim notes, "At first, the voice may start out small, with just a whisper. But as it grows louder, so will your discontent. Don't ignore how you feel—it just may mean you're onto something real. When you can no longer ignore that inner voice pointing you toward a new path, it's time to listen" (Peak Wellbeing, 2016).

It turns out my mom was onto something. She had brought into my life the gift of learning how to be truly grounded in my own purpose, going so much deeper into what I thought I knew. Life with purpose is not just about crushing a half marathon, making your goals at work, or even helping your kid get into college. Yes, these feed your ego and have a short-term, surface-level effect. Visible goals are important, but they aren't feeding your soul or tapping into your purpose. The invisible, under the surface, and higher goals are even more important, if not more so.

Kim sums it up like this: "Once your business is established and thriving, don't be afraid to continue dreaming."

During the time I lost my voice, I rethought my business. I knew I needed to ReLaunch it—along with myself—so the company could expand into the new opportunities coming forward. I was in the process of evolving my new identity to the person who would have everything I was looking to create. I wanted to be in prime ReLaunch shape to put my new podcast out there in thirty days or less.

Clarity is the key to manifestation, so I developed a specific plan as opposed to a general goal and focused on having the best people in the industry help me. Next, I set a success metric of the target number of downloads within that first month. I started to visualize myself speaking into the mic, and I could see my audience listening to it. The brain, meanwhile, not differentiating between a visualization and reality, assumes what I'm thinking is already real, and it wants to deliver that scenario, doing everything it can to try to make my vision come to life. I continued to use new, even more specific affirmations, and my morning mantra was feeling more natural daily. I was living the ReLaunch daily affirmation.

What I was thinking on the inside was showing up on the outside in real life.

Within twenty-three days—with the help of Michelle Abraham from *AmplifYou Voice*—I launched a podcast that hit every single one of the metrics I had put out there as my objectives. To keep on track with my sense of purpose, four or five times a day I would go through this movie in my mind and state my intentions. I began by living, feeling, and thinking like a person who would have a successful powerhouse podcast. I was super clear on the future vision and who I needed to be to make it happen. I hit all my pre-set goals—including being in the top 2.5 percent of all podcasts in the world—and it all started by writing down clearly what I wanted and my "why" behind it.

The Power of Your Pen

Do you have a time machine? You just might. At age sixty-two, Oprah Winfrey decided to write something personal: a letter to her forty-two-year-old self. She wrote, "You spent too many days and years trying to please other people and be what they wanted you to be." She wished she had been able to give herself permission to release—after all these challenges, successes, and years—who she really was (Winfrey, 2021).

In the late 1980s, when she had a successful, Chicago-based talk show, Oprah took on the critical 3HQ™ question of *who am I*. The show was a huge success with the TV network executives. The problem for Oprah was their definition of success was a programming formula across multiple shows that thrived on exploitation—shock-surprise interviews with women whose husbands admitted to sleeping with their sister, for example, or interviewing women who had had children with their fathers ("Oprah Evolves," n.d.). This

was, in fact, a popular talk show format at the time, and hosts vied to shock their audiences. Ratings soared, but Oprah did not feel comfortable. She was not successful according to the definition of *who* she wanted to be. This is often an early sign your heart and head are not working together. She began pushing her boundaries exploring other creative options.

A colleague of mine was present in the late 1980s at a meeting with Oprah, her attorney, and the president of her TV network when Oprah gave a pitch for a new TV show she hoped to produce and star in.

The network president was patronizing. He suggested Oprah had enough to keep her busy as it was. Oprah sat silently, politely fuming, but she made her displeasure known. Her chair was beneath a huge Ficus tree. My colleague described how Oprah reached up and started plucking leaves off the tree. At that point, when the network president mispronounced Oprah's name (he called her "Oh-pree"), she pulled down a small branch.

After the meeting, Oprah and her team huddled outside the building with her attorney, who said, "You've got this, Oprah. You'll be producing your own show." He told my colleague Oprah had purchased her own production studio, putting her own money on the line, and was renovating it to house her entire staff. The network would have no control over her future because she would be syndicating the show herself, along with other independent partners. Bye-bye, network. They would now have to come to her. The network president passing on her show concept was a disappointment, but it gave her a way to find her real niche, stay true to herself, and become who she knew she would be.

In 1989, Oprah formed her own production company, Harpo. She announced she was changing her format, taking a U-turn, and rebranding her talk show to focus on positivity and self-improvement. She was leaning into her authentic self: a woman who could connect and communicate with others and add values in scarce supply in the entertainment industry at the time.

Was this a risky ReLaunch, even for a successful celebrity? Yes. A huge and potentially devastatingly costly risk to Oprah's career. Nobody else on daytime TV was doing anything even close to this. No woman star since Lucille Ball had announced she was building her own TV studio and certainly no woman of color.

History has proved Oprah's intuition was correct.

When you feel you're out of options, it's easy to close the door and resign yourself to your situation instead of looking for possibilities while keeping the door open, understanding the messages that lie within. Your 3HQ™ is off balance. Maybe, like Oprah, you're in a dream job, but it's making you uncomfortable. Maybe, like Shona, you have a dream but need to close the gap between it and what you are doing in real life. It's time to readjust and

accept the risk and the responsibility to connect the dots and move forward into the energy source of your Higher Self.

It was 9 p.m. on a Saturday night when Liani Kotcher decided to drop in on her husband, a security expert, who was in the midst of weeks of high-stakes, back-to-back, twenty-four- seven litigation meetings. Having been a top lawyer herself, Kotcher knew the territory and knew he could use a break. Trying to stay below the radar, she sidled into the "war room" area (and flashed on a throwback scene from her own days as a top intellectual property attorney). She found an entire team on lockdown; her husband, five parties glued to various phones, strategy and deposition paperwork stacked to the ceiling, boxes of dead pizzas and empty soft drink cans. Backing out of the room, Kotcher went directly home, opened a book to research her latest plot, and smiled as feelings of gratitude washed over her. *Thank God*, she thought, *I no longer do that.*

Now an award-winning author of a successful series of young adult novels, Kotcher leaped off the hamster wheel of college, law school, top law firm, crazy hours, and seven-day weeks. "I took showers with my Blackberry. I had a top-paying job and sexy, front-page cases. I was crushing it," she says. "But I was a prisoner of the golden handcuffs; the money and the super comfortable life were so tempting." She also had a creative side rumbling under the surface. She had been an avid reader since childhood and her passion was writing, but her parents had always told her it was not a viable career path. Still, she had always longed to be a storyteller. Was there any hope? Did she have the courage to go for her passion? Would she make the biggest mistake of her life?

"I began with baby steps," she said.

Kotcher took writing classes for two years, writing on the side.

I met Kotcher when she moved to California. She told me she felt her inner purpose was to tell stories, but she didn't know how to make this ReLaunch. In fact, she had a deep fear—a fear of being an impostor. How could she call herself a writer? We decided to work together to sort out her mindset and her childhood B.U.G. that was telling her she would never make it as a writer.

"So much of my identity was tied up in being a lawyer," she said. "Saying 'I'm a writer'—I felt like I didn't own that for such a long time. To move forward, I think it's important to find someone who holds you accountable, or it's too easy to get off track as you make a transition. I just kept moving forward, step by step. This changed my life. I built up a skill set and learned to believe in myself." Once she embraced her inner truth and sense of purpose, Kotcher had the inner foundation to not only become a writer, but for future ReLaunches as well.

Today, Kotcher is not only an award-winning writer of a successful, critically appraised young adult thriller book series, but also a literary blogger, influencer, coach, and consultant, focusing on being a go-to resource on the business aspects of launching a writing career.

"I found my higher power truth," she says. "Now I love connecting with other people, helping them to live their passion."

Transitions are times of change, and right now, it seems the entire world is in a tsunami-like transition and most of us are swept along in it, along with our own inevitable transitions. As in the case of Liani Kotcher, your identity—how you see yourself and how others see you—may be shifting. Transitions are when you step up and say, "I will not let circumstances be in control of who I am. I can only control the controllable."

Although it's easy in such a situation to feel like so much is out of your control, it's never too late to focus on a positive outcome and the potential new self-image you hope to create. To do so, you need to be clear and believe, deep inside, that you are already what you want to be. Jim Fortin says:

> *There are two different types of identity. One identity is assured and confident; the other works from circumstance. The first identity creates your world; the second identity is being molded by it. If your negative thoughts show up in encounters with others, they*

will feel it. Instead, you have to manage the energy you bring to any situation—be it a date, an interview, a sales pitch, a relationship, or bringing up a child. This starts by changing your thoughts—and then beliefs change.

When you accept 100 percent responsibility for your life, you can change what you believe about yourself and the world. Oprah said, "Only you have the responsibility to move your life forward. The sooner you get that, the sooner your life gets into gear. It does not matter where you come from. It doesn't matter your circumstances. What matters is this moment and what you're willing to do right now" (Mindspo, 2020).

You can't say Oprah just "won the lottery." Anyone who struggled through the traumatic life circumstances of her early years—including childhood sexual abuse and the death of an illegitimate child who was born and died shortly after birth when she was only fourteen years old—certainly does not fit that qualification. Even as a young person, she had the strength of character to flip the dialogue. "I viewed it as my second chance," she said (Johnson, 2011). Instead, she made the lottery come to her on her terms—and everybody won. Having struggled her way up through the byzantine, male-dominated hierarchies of the entertainment industry, Oprah Winfrey succeeded and literally changed, first, her own namesake show, and then the landscape of American media (Medium, 2018).

By being true to herself and pivoting her business platform—and daring to go against the conventional "wisdom"—Oprah opened a window connecting with an entire nation of followers. She channeled her higher, best self and—by being authentic to who she was—brought out the best in us. By raising her energy level out of blame and shame and focusing on a higher level of love, joy, and peace, she raised our energy as we watched her and

impacted something even deeper: our culture. That's the 3HQ™ Effect operating efficiently. It's Heart, Head, and Higher Self working in total alignment, creating a ripple effect from the nucleus of one person's totally aligned inner vision to a community level.

Perhaps even more significantly, Oprah opened the door for a public shepherding of a mass audience to celebrate diversity and differences among people. Today, this seems almost the status quo, but at the time, it was a unique breakthrough. Oprah broke down the color and cultural lines not just for herself, but for her audience. She knew it was not okay to just be like-minded. Taking it to the next level of like-minded viewers required what I call *like energy.* Alignment, it turns out, is not one-size-fits-all.

Recent research has shown the culture we participate in plays a powerful role in our individual self-identity. The impact is symbiotic (Science Direct, 2021). This perspective is a departure from centuries of thought that assumed our emotions were hardwired from our primitive DNA and therefore singular, unchangeable neuropathways. From the ancient times of Plato, it was assumed that any shift in emotion was not due to an actual change but rather from a kind of ongoing "battle with the brain," where the mind stepped in to counteract or disable fixed emotion. In her impactful book, *How*

Emotions Are Made: The Secret Life of the Brain, Lisa Feldman Barrett, PhD, reports on more recent, contradictory findings that impact how we see not only the emotion/mind equation, but the role of culture: "Emotions are not universal but vary from culture to culture. They emerge as a combination of the physical properties of your body, a flexible brain that wires itself to whatever environment it develops in, and your culture and upbringing, which provide that environment" (Barrett, 2017).

If alignment is the key to unity, we must understand the components of the culture, beginning with all those environmental factors that contribute to the 3HQ™. The energy of the Heart is not generic; a spectrum maps to all emotions. The 3HQ™ is the roadway that allows you to take the next step, to navigate and elevate that frequency. However, it's not just presumptuous, but inaccurate to assume we all get onto that freeway from the same place.

Neuroscience has tracked this "energy trail" by assigning levels to the spectrum, like the rungs of a ladder. At the bottom are low vibrational levels as when you are probably not liking yourself very much, possibly feeling depressed, scattered, or even self-sabotaging, while blaming circumstances and seeing yourself as a victim (see Calamity Hilary Jayne). If we hope to be aligned with a higher sense of purpose—or a value like a better job or healthier relationship, which would emanate its own higher vibrational level—then we have to work on ourselves to clear the way to climb up the spectrum to get there. A low energy level, like sadness, will only attract other low-energy-level entities.

This applies to things as well as people. For instance, foods have been classified on the vibration spectrum. The source, quality, and intention of how the food was grown all impact its vibration and energy level. Organic, unprocessed, locally sourced vegetables and fruits that have been grown in the earth have high vibration while processed foods like white breads or additive-heavy foods have low vibration levels. These lack the nutrition and energy benefits of higher-vibration foods, like organic vegetables (Starseed Kitchen, 2020). A human connection also transfers the vibration level.

Even the attitude of the person who is preparing the food has an impact on the dish. The neuro-kitchen is not far in the future; in fact, it is already here. Multi-star chefs tout their use of high vibration foods, which represents a "cultural shift." Just as we are able to choose our food to raise our level of energy, we are able to choose our thoughts in order to raise the quality of our lives (Jean-Georges, 2021). Celebrity chef Michael Lyon said, "I literally need to get into an energy state of positivity so I put that into everything I cook."

Whether we watch Oprah, *60 Minutes*, subtitled global streaming, or anything digital, we have all participated. We are all part of a collective where culture and community feed off each other and participate in the raising and lowering of our vibration and energy levels.

The Hybrid relaunch

Are rumblings of discontent about your work at the core of your ReLaunch? If so, you're far from alone (Baumgartner, 2020). The "Great Resignation" phenomenon has reflected the numbing impact of a global low-vibration scenario that has given the entire work universe a gut punch, leaving it reeling. In addition to the droves of workers leaving or switching jobs, the hybrid work model has resulted in an unplanned but evolving challenge to our identities. A PwC survey conducted in 2021 states nine thousand respondents identified a gap "between employer expectations and employee preferences." Over a third of executives said the loss of corporate culture was "the biggest challenge to hybrid work." According to the survey, 65 percent of the respondents were looking for new jobs in 2021. Fewer than half of those were leaving for reasons of higher pay.

For as long as anyone can remember, the elevator question has been, "Where do you work?" What you said immediately conjured up an image of who you were—the trappings of your tribe. However, if you choose to work from home, exactly who is that tribe, and where can they be found? Hey, you in the upper left-hand square on my screen, let's meet for a latte in the metaverse? Are you still included in a work culture, and how? If you are an entrepreneur, do you see your identity differently than someone working for a corporation? How is work-versus-home culture maintained in a work-*from*-home world—or a hybrid one, where professional and home lives overlap? If we have choices, which will we choose and why?

On the other side of the screen, employers are suddenly invited into our homes on an ongoing basis via video conferencing. They've become virtual guests of our

families. Not that long ago corporate women were nervous about putting family pictures on their desks, while today your toddler's highchair—or the toddlers themselves—may be onscreen in your 10 a.m. video call. Although, as Yogi Berra once noted, "Predictions are risky, especially when they're about the future," it's fairly safe to predict your coworkers are probably going to be watching your kids grow up—and you theirs—in the background of some sort of device for years to come (Cannon, 2017).

In this way, yet another kind of community has formed, blurring professional and personal borders. It is now officially impossible to "leave your work at the office." As a popular coffee commercial that showed a company team convening on a Zoom video call—with one man's misplaced angle revealing his underwear and bare legs below his business shirt—sang in its jingle: "Your whole team can see your upper thigh, so aim that camera high ..." (Folgers, 2021). They see London, they see France, they can see your underpants.

Today, we are the first generation of Hybrid ReLaunchers, the intrepid explorers, the front- line Magellans of the virtual-slash-IRL (in-real-life) community. Undeniably, we face fresh challenges, but we are going to the "new different." We are proactively looking and moving forward. We entrepreneurs are the mapmakers of our own future. We who work with or for organizations are leading the way as well because the work of the future is being reconfigured around us, as opposed to the opposite (which is, thankfully, being left in the rearview mirror). The Head alone is not equipped to optimize this journey. Our knowledge, however encyclopedic, can't cross this new frontier. Today, we must lead from the Heart, where emotion, culture, and affinity reside.

The 3HQ™ is critical to the new Hybrid ReLaunch, digital versus bricks and mortar. Virtual versus IRL are methods of delivery, not values. Dress codes are uniforms, not the people inside them. The Hybrid ReLaunch is likewise about a new recognition and awareness of the spectrum of values of who we are. These are our values, encompassing those of the individuals who are the mother lode of our ideas, the engine driving the work, the makers and masters of their craft. That craft could be a boiled egg, a suture, a garden, a quarterly accountability report, twenty-six perfect pirouettes, a clean street, a haircut, an animal's shelter, a propulsion rocket to Mars, a chord in a cathedral, a hand-thrown pot, or a swaddling blanket tucked just so—an infinity of examples. Each contributor to the blockchain of these entities brings to it their values, which imbue the work itself with a vibration of energy, even if it is inanimate. We who do the work are the essences, the sources of the energy that we send out into the world and share—for a price.

In this new hybrid world, we have found ourselves asking if the value received is worth the energy we have given. If an alignment is not there, the machinery of the transaction breaks down. Today's leaders must examine the 3HQ™ within themselves and lead by example before they can develop the culture their company will follow.

Today, when we open those doors inside us, we must not use a flashlight to illuminate what we see, but a full-on searchlight. We can no longer paste labels on the values and check the boxes. As a transformational coach, I have become humbled by this. I know my experiences have been limited to privilege. My reality TV experience with homelessness, for instance, is at best superficial compared to the depth of the issues. Writing this book has helped me recognize this and realize the ReLaunch journey I thought it would take me on was not the journey it has become. I speak of like-minded energy, but I recognize my energy and someone else's—less privileged and with fewer advantages—would have their own limiting beliefs far different than mine. Until the terrain and history has been leveled to a far greater degree, significant additional work must be done.

Dr. Brenda Wade, says:

> *Your heart will take you where the head can't—vibrating at the same frequency as other beings of the heart. But even if it looks like their journey is one of people who look like you, when the core values come out, you don't know that they are like you.*

She related a story of teaching at a preschool where certain assumptions might have been made about her due to her education and the current environment:

> *But those people had no idea, while they could afford to pay for a high-end preschool for their children, I had no money, was a starving grad student, and was eating the kids' leftover fruit cups and pudding cups from snack time as my food. Differences must be clear and acknowledged in order for alignment to come together in the workforce.*

I'm reminded of a young man who grew up with the kids of one of my clients. He's now in his thirties and vice president of a major investment bank. Growing up, he was on scholarships. Today, although some might not be surprised to learn he was raised by a struggling single mother who was a nurse, few would imagine his father has been in prison for murder for his son's entire life. His limiting beliefs might be quite different from others at the investment bank. As a young person of a different skin color, he fit in smoothly, and my client always admired him for that. One wonders what that obviously hard-won alignment must have cost him—on the inside. He's now had decades of practice at success dynamics, but what might it cost him today?

There's no Band-Aid for the soul. Dr. Wade emphasizes other souls—i.e., we—"[reach] out behind us to bring forward those millions who will follow."

As employers, work colleagues, fellow entrepreneurs, and humans, we won't solve these issues without taking the first step to move beyond assumptions and into awareness. It's a beginning. The old platitudes won't cut it. They will no longer suffice when the stakes are so high that an entire workforce is on the line. Note to the corporate community: when that tipping point goes over the edge, it's not coming back, even if you offer them a month's paid

vacation. If you are the person going over that edge, you need to be prepared with a full arsenal of awareness. That's where the 3HQ™ Method comes in as a tool for inner change management. Just bringing these invisible issues to the surface is a step in itself.

Change is not just fluid, it's breakneck out of control. Sometimes it looks like a straight line, while sometimes it's a squiggly line and, not infrequently, it looks like a fireworks explosion. It's normal for change to be something you may want but just can't have, access, or see right now. You may have it, lose it, then reignite it. Allow yourself to embrace and be grateful for, rather than fear, the freedom. If you take even one small step forward, you're on the change train and no longer stuck. You are headed for your transformation (Glaser, 2019).

QUESTIONS TO THINK ABOUT:

1. What do you feel your Highest Self's true purpose is? Are you living that true purpose, and if not, why not?
2. What unique talents do you have that can help you move closer to living your purpose in the new hybrid world?
3. What B.U.G.S. from the questions in previous chapters can you replace to find better health, wealth, and relationships?

PART FOUR

THE G-ZONE: GRATITUDE AND GRACE

CHAPTER TWELVE

VISIBLE GRATITUDE

As I'm at my computer, writing this chapter on a work-day Sunday, I'm looking straight out at the spectacular Boulder landscape—huge, snow-capped trees, bright-blue sky, the horizon of downtown Boulder. And just in front of my window, a buck with antlers strolling with his doe- eyed girlfriend. I love the beauty and magnificence of this place and feel a surge of gratitude for the fact that I took the chance to uproot and relocate here after being a lifetime California girl. Rumbles in my stomach have just emerged, and I'm edging on a tinge of regret for not being able to be outside skiing or joining in the fun, when suddenly, I see Erich walking toward my office with a plate in his hand.

His timing couldn't be any better. No, what was better was the warm panini, oozing cheese, sautéed veggies, and even turkey bacon—with a crunchy side of homemade sweet potato fries. Lunch was served! Once upon a time, I might have said something like, "That's so great; put it on the desk and give me a moment to finish up these pages …" Instead, I took a breath and leaned into the moment. I hit the pause button, stopped what I was doing, looked at him, and let him visibly know how much I appreciated this act of kindness. I felt gratitude for being in this place, at this time, with my life partner, had just multiplied tenfold. Maybe the way to my heart is through my mouth, but at this moment, I am the happiest, most grateful person on earth.

It's funny how timing works in your life. Just when you could use it, happiness arrives in the form of a warm panini. Now, if you could only make that stick. Small acts gratitude and gratefulness like this create a boomerang effect. Erich got visible recognition, and I got the panini.

Acts and actions like the warm panini create an impact zone on the doer and the giver that emanates an energy field surrounding both, like a halo effect.

The power of visible gratitude is limitless. In the case of Sara Blakely, founder of SPANX shapewear for women, two years before the phenomenal deal that made her one of the world's richest women, Blakely posted something on Instagram, following a long-haul international flight—which included a picture of herself with the flight attendant. Bored with her iPod playlist, she had found herself listening to a motivational podcast. That's when the magic happened.

Here's her Instagram post:

> *I spend the next two hours listening about the power of positive mindset and how our thoughts create energy around us. I turn the iPod off and create positive thoughts. I start with gratitude and start listing all the things I'm grateful for. Then I start sending love*

and positive energy out to everyone on the plane. I visualize them all happy and fulfilled. I wish the best for them.

Eventually, the flight attendant comes up to me. She said, "Excuse me, I have a gift for you." It was a green stone from Madagascar that represents peace and harmony. I got chills. We truly receive what we put out into the universe. Our thoughts are powerful. They not only affect our lives, but the lives of those around us. I have been using the power of thought throughout my life, and especially throughout my SPANX® journey. So, the next time you find yourself bored, sad, angry, irritated ... start with gratitude. Shift to sending love and healing out into the world and see what happens.

What could you do with kindergarten scissors and a pair of control-top pantyhose? Do you think you could create a billion-dollar business within twelve years? In 2000, Sara Blakely thought so. She cut the legs off the pantyhose, put up a bankroll of five thousand dollars of her own money, and launched a revolution—a women's shapewear business that, by 2012, made her the world's youngest self-made female billionaire and one of *Time*'s one hundred most influential people. Within ten years, SPANX announced an agreement for a majority investment by a leading global financial company who bought a majority stake at a valuation of $1.2 billion (Business Wire, 2021).

"When I first started SPANX," said Blakely, "I wrote a goal down and I said this company will one day be worth twenty million dollars, and everybody laughed at me, and you know,

I said I really believe that." That in itself is an incredible accomplishment—of both business and manifestation—but the mission-driven values behind it is an even more amazing story.

SPANX, which calls itself a brand that is "by women, for women," has a very specific mission. According to its website, "We believe women can do anything. And together, we believe we will make the world a better place … one butt at a time!"

> "We believe women can do anything. And together, we believe we will make the world a better place... *one butt at a time!*"
>
> SARAH BLAKELY

Blakely celebrated the deal in what has been called "spectacularly generous fashion," gifting every one of her seven hundred-fifty employees, including the janitorial staff, two first-class plane tickets to travel anywhere in the world along with ten thousand dollars in cash to spend however they please.

"This is a very big moment for each and every one of you," Blakely announced on her Instagram account. "To stand here today and think about what we've been able to create and what we've been able to do by being authentic and kind and delivering amazing products to women to use their very feminine principles in a very masculine space which is business, leading with intuition and vulnerability ... This marks a moment for female entrepreneurs" (Blakely, 2021).

Blakely's mission of creating a culture of gratitude is a straight-through line from the SPANX workplace community to the customer and onto the world we all inhabit. It's this consistency that fuels its authenticity. SPANX delivers on their stated mission ("Our Purpose: Elevating Women," 2021).

The Panini Effect

Similar to intuition, gratitude is an amazing value because it encompasses every thought, emotion, and sense—the entire 3HQ™ arc is enlisted and impacted. For instance, we know something as simple as expressing appreciation is a way to show visible gratitude—I'm naming it the Panini Effect. And however you choose to show gratitude—whether invisibly with a feeling or visibly with a helping hand, a smile, a note, or a check—your reward can be a thousand-fold.

"A massive game-changer" is how YouTube video marketing innovator, business coach of Business by Design, and host of the *Mind Your Business* podcast James Wedmore refers to it.

> *"Gratitude is an emotional state you feel when you're in a certain vibrational frequency. Just like you're tuning a radio dial to a station, you're tuning into this particular state, or level, of gratitude."*
>
> *Gratitude is the state you feel when you're receiving. We put our attention on the current circumstance of our life—the here and now in this moment. We see*

what we have. And then we see what we don't. Maybe we log into our bank account, we see what we have, we see what we don't have; we look at our Instagram following, and we see how many followers we have. And if they don't see what they want, in this moment, most people tend to say, "Oh, it's not enough. It's not what I want." And that will definitely trail away from gratitude.

Wedmore acknowledges realization can be the start of a ReLaunch toward something that will take them to a more productive and rewarding level of success.

A lot of times, life gives you some of the greatest opportunities and invitations for your best life possible—but they're disguised. It's up to you to see the good, to see the opportunity, and to be grateful for it.

By flipping your perspective, you create a newly uncovered space for a positive outcome. The ReLaunch Flip could be the gateway to your higher sense of purpose and spark new momentum toward, say, a successful entrepreneurial venture or next corporate promotion. For instance, if an expected promotion, bonus, raise, or opportunity does not come through, instead of stewing in inertia, you have the chance to look sideways, up, and down to perhaps make a shift in another direction, department, or field to bring you into that lifestyle of success, however you define it.

Operating in gratitude is a two-way street. Erich and I both felt great about the panini—he who made it, I who ate it—so it's no surprise to me that gratitude has been documented as positively correlated to greater happiness (Brower, 2021). A sense of gratitude releases dopamine and serotonin, neurotransmitters responsible for positive mood-enhancing emotions—the feel-good guys (Chowdhury, 2022).

Research on gratitude at Cornell University suggests people who express gratitude on a regular basis have higher levels of optimism, physical well-being, and determination ("The Gratitude Project," 2018). It's a domino effect.

"Identifying the benefits you get from the good things in your life provides a positive impact on the way you think and feel about yourself, others, and even your challenges," said Cornell Graduate School's Associate Dean of Academic and Student Affairs Jan Allen ("The Gratitude Project," 2018).

What could be a greater gift than one where you receive many times more than you give? Energy, vitality, enthusiasm—it turns out, they're all ingredients in that panini ("Giving

Thanks Can Make You Happier," 2021).

Start simple. Notice everything around you; be aware of the simple things. What makes you feel good? The blue sky, the sun on your face, the smile on a loved one's face? These kinds of things are gratefulness triggers that make us feel good, and the more we are mindful and take notice of them, the more they become self-reinforcing gratitude habits (Frontiers, 2021).

This is where flipping the script is not unlike taking the fruit instead of the chips. "When you practice gratitude, you are distracted from worries and other negative emotions," Jan

Allen notes. "In tough times and adversity, rather than focus on the negative, leaning into what you can be grateful for can help pull you through" (Emmons, 2013).

Dr. Robert A. Emmons, PhD, who has been called "the Father of Gratitude," is the world's leading scientific expert on the topic. He notes a key reason why gratitude has never been more important or relevant. "In moments of downturn and loss, gratitude becomes a critical cognitive process—a way of thinking about the world that can help us turn disaster into a steppingstone," he explains (Emmons, 2013).

I'm reminded again of my mom's ability to synthesize and convert negatives to positives—how a little room became a big view, and no walls became no limits.

She nailed it again.

The New Bottom Line for Business

"While showing gratitude has always been important for leaders ... it may be the most essential thing you can do right now—for very pragmatic reasons," says Chester Elton, author of the 2020 book *Leading with Gratitude.* "In the ever-tighter talent market CEOs are now facing, hanging on to great people is everything. And when it comes to retention, gratitude is the most powerful tool available—far more so than money."

Today more than ever, retention of talent has become an emotional as well as financial proposition. Elton, who has spent twenty years studying corporate culture, points out, "You don't leave people who love you ... The number one reason people leave a job is the relationship with their immediate supervisor. If you want turnover, don't use gratitude. If you want people to stay, let them know they matter" (Bigman and Buss, 2021).

Even before the cataclysmic upheaval of the pandemic, a shift had begun in workplace dynamics. In 2019, Eric Mosley noted in the *Forbes* article "The Impact of Gratitude," a movement "toward a more human workplace, rooted in gratitude, where employees feel appreciated, valued, respected, and empowered to reach their fullest potential." This, in turn, triggered "happiness, well-being, morale, energy, and engagement—all of which directly influence performance, productivity, and retention" (Mosley, 2019).

In "The Remarkable Power of Gratitude," Dan Bigman and Dale Buss report on promising corporate gratitude scenarios. One company's executive team set up an internal chat channel where they have a chance to share gratitude with each other. Another company stressed gratitude in their daily morning meetings, including a slide called "Grateful Appreciations." A "Kudos" section on the internal website provides a chance for another company's team members to thank or appreciate one another. Many companies celebrate employees with a social or virtual event, like a holiday party. But can gratitude be monetized? Some say yes. A version of this involves empowering supervisors to share their bonuses with their teams (Bigman and Buss, 2021).

However, showing gratitude and sharing the impact doesn't need to involve money. For instance, people who sent written notes of thanks displayed significantly better mental health than those who didn't. A study of gratitude letter-writing among college students also suggested better mental health was possibly indicated by a sort of mental bait-and-switch tactic—a ReLaunch Flip of sorts—that shift one's attention away from toxic emotions, such as resentment and envy, to focus on something deserving of gratitude (Brown and Wong, 2017).

Philanthropic organizations are on the front line regarding the impact of writing gratitude letters as part of fundraising initiatives. "I think you have to touch people in the heart," says Mary Ann Barnes, board chair of ARC (Activities, Recreation, and Care for Individuals with Intellectual and Developmental Disabilities) in the Greater Los Angeles Area ("About," 2021). "We wrote a handwritten thank-you appeal to every person who had previously given or had a relative in the program. I think that shows. It comes through we care—because we do. People can feel that."

Barnes's adult brother participates in the program, so she and her family have a personal interest. For example, after reaching out to a previous donor with a note that mentioned a shared emotional incident, the man then called to say he was leaving his estate to the organization.

"People want to be a part of something good and see the learning, the life-long friendships, and the stories of where their gifts are going; they want to feel the connection," she says, noting, on the other hand, a straightforward fundraising video did not have much impact. "We followed that up with a heartfelt appeal letter—and a hundred donations flooded in. You can have heart and still make good business decisions. Today, I wrote thirteen thank-you notes."

The corporate community is just beginning to scratch the surface of the potential or the power of gratitude to go beyond the world of "the soft stuff" to a business tool with profit potential. An Oakland, California, research study revealed companies with a focus on employee recognition were twelve times more likely to create positive business outcomes, yet only 20 percent of organizations are using an effective employee recognition program. The gratitude-forward CEO, however, is far from alone in the crowd. A 2021 CEO survey reported

in *Forbes* revealed that 90 percent of CEOs surveyed feel it is important to "lead with gratitude" (Borysenko, 2019). If gratefulness is the value, the issue is taking the action step to close the gap between belief and doing. You can use the 3HQ™ Method to both defocus on the negatives and potential dead ends of a business and become more optimistically aware of where opportunities might appear. Gratitude has a way of stacking the deck in your favor. Have you considered writing a note of gratitude to somebody today?

The New Power Paradigm

Brain scans suggest gratitude might even have the power to rewire our brains for the better. As mentioned, when we express and receive gratitude, our brain releases two "feel good" chemicals: dopamine and serotonin. These two crucial neurotransmitters are responsible for our emotions. Their impact on the body is to release feelings of happiness. Habits and rituals that reinforce gratitude daily, such as keeping a gratitude journal, can help strengthen neural pathways through repetitive actions and ultimately change our mood to an overall state of appreciation and gratitude (Neurohealth Associates, 2020).

Alexsys Thompson is a best-selling author, keynote speaker, creator of two gratitude journals, and the Gratitude 540 brand, which includes journals that focus on specific life areas to support the journey into gratitude. She links gratitude to potential leadership in *The* ReLaunch *Podcast* episode "If You Lead a Life, You Are a Leader." Her book, *The Power of a Graceful Leader*, redefines the integrated qualities of leadership—in life and in business—that align perfectly with the 3HQ™ platform:

> *This pathway will assist you in becoming fully present to your purpose, your strengths, and the choices you have in front of you to help you step into becoming the leader you dream of being. As you open new ways of seeing and interfacing with the world around you, new possibilities will become available to you. Gratitude is the virtue that sets up and opens the door for every other virtue. Gratitude covers the whole spectrum of human emotion—it's not just one thing. In no way does gratitude sugarcoat the tough stuff in our lives.*

It's not all goody-two-shoes, however. If things are negative, if something is not good—an illness, for instance—you are open to acknowledge that. In these cases, gratitude can be a lifesaver. The negative brick in the pavement can be acknowledged as foundational, and then we move on and build the wall. It's okay to grieve or acknowledge things could be better, and then, as Thompson puts it, "throw a rope over the wall" and pull yourself out by practicing gratitude. This is, in fact, fundamental to the skill sets needed for ReLaunchability and flipping the script. Through this lens, potential failure morphs from challenge to opportunity.

What this process does is give you complete access without shutting down any part of the 3HQ™. It's acknowledgment, not denial. "If you can't change something or you can't modify it, accept it with grace and move on," stresses Thompson. "When something is fundamentally changing, we can't go back to the old ways. We won't."

QUESTIONS TO THINK ABOUT:

1. When was the last time someone gave you a warm panini? When was the last time you gave one to someone else?
2. What is a warm panini you have ignored or not shown proper gratitude for in the last week? How can you make that situation better starting right now?
3. What is stopping you from using the 3HQ™ Method to make your life better? What would living the 3HQ™ life change or improve for you?

CHAPTER THIRTEEN

RELAUNCH RESILIENCE

Sometimes we look at high-profile people and think, *Wow, they've got it so easy! No wonder they're a success.* But the truth is, like many of us, they're usually not dissimilar to ducks, floating seemingly placidly on the glassy surface while paddling madly beneath the waterline.

When something negative happens to you, do you bounce back or get beaten down? Resilience is our talent for adapting well, for bouncing back quickly from adversity or trauma ("Building Your Resilience," 2012). Research on resilience has shown people who are exhibiting resilience through life's challenges and transitions are also those who have a strong sense of purpose.

What kind of resilience does it take to go from figure skating to homelessness to (while you're at it) making your own film on homelessness on your iPhone to the red carpet at the Oscars? To founding and running your own social-impact production company and mentoring academy?

Cali Gilbert is an inspiring, real-world example of a phoenix manifesting her journey toward abundance and gratitude.

Having spent her early life in competitive figure skating, and with a fresh master's degree in management in hand, Cali formed an event management consulting firm supporting the nonprofit sector. Yet when the recession hit, her world fell apart, including losing her home. From that unenviable position, Cali executed a masterful ReLaunch Flips, one that took her literally from a storage warehouse to couch-surfing on a San Francisco houseboat to the red carpet. Cali and I had a conversation on *The* ReLaunch *Podcast* about being homeless, how she coped, and how that came full circle to almost unimaginable success—and gratitude.

"I've often said I feel like I've lived about nine lifetimes just this time around," Cali said, "because I've done so much and accomplished so much, and I've gone through so much transformation. But it's been a blessing. It really has. When I look back at it now, it's like, yes. Thank you. Thank you. Thank you for all of it, even in those moments when it was deep despair, because it really has made me who I am today. And I am definitely grateful for that."

I asked how she managed all these transitions from athlete, to publisher, to filmmaker.

"In 2011, I literally lost everything—beginning with losing a child. My relationship ended, my car died, my money ran out, and ultimately, I lost my home," Cali explained. "I ended up spending twelve months homeless in the San Francisco Bay area and really needed to decide what I wanted my life to look like. I was at a point where I had a decision to make, and that was do I start over, or do I give up? And I thought, well, as an artist, I feel if I start over, I've got this blank canvas. So, what is it I want my life to look like? And within a few months, I was able to completely turn my life around."

She continued, "I believe there's this stereotype around homelessness—it only happens to those who are criminals or mentally ill or drug addicts. And that's just not true. This could happen to anyone, even someone like me with multiple degrees. Career counselors advised me to yank my degrees off my resume and 'dumb it down.'"

"*How was this happening to me? Why, why, why?*" she asked. "Looking back [on her two separate bouts of homelessness] it was interesting to see my mental state at that point. The first time, as opposed to the second time, when I thought, *Well, you know what, I didn't die the first time, so I know I'm going to be okay. So let's look at this with a different mindset.* That really taught me the power of setting those intentions of what I wanted to create, and the life I wanted. As this was all happening, I lost a child. I was going through the grief period. That began the house of cards falling. By September 2011, the money was running out and I was barely holding onto my home. Nothing was working."

She turned to creative outlets—writing and photography, hobbies she'd always enjoyed but never practiced professionally—and produced a book of photographs and inspirational quotes of the life she hoped to create for herself. Cali decided to take advantage of an invitation to a book marketing conference in San Diego. Trading helping with the event for her entrance fee, it allowed her to go spend three days in San Diego and learn from the best of the publishing industry.

Thirty days later, in the midst of losing everything, Cali self-published her first book.

"It was amazing to see how things were lining up, once I became in alignment with what I was truly meant to do. I totally believe the body tells us when we're out of alignment with life," she says. "Every day, I was in tears due to a serious back injury because my job at the warehouse was so stressful and involved heavy lifting. I was popping painkillers like candy and I thought, *I'm going to die any day now.* I eventually lost my job because I couldn't work. And of course, that job was my home—the apartment came with the job.

"But that moment was when I had the mind shift, and it was: *I will not die. I'm going to be okay.* Instead of looking at it from that survival victim mentality, I'm going to look at it as if

I'm on an adventure. Why not? From there, I published four books in one year.

"After the first time things fell apart, when I was at that point of no return, I asked myself, *Do I give up, do I start over?* What I did was set the intention for the three things I wanted. And they were very simple things: I wanted to stay in Sausalito, I wanted to find a part-time job that paid the bills and allowed me to do what I loved, and I wanted to wake each day and create via my writing and photography. Within two and a half months, I had manifested all of it.

"Anything is possible," Cali says. "We've got these incredible gifts we should be able to share with the world. Manifesting gratitude is about this amplification, this idea you're just turning up the volume of gratitude. And it's such an awesome state."

Later, as a former homeless producer and now a filmmaker, Gilbert has a unique, first-person perspective and insight into such intimate aspects of this world, which helped make her film a global award-winner and a Masterclass in the ReLaunch Flip (Lebsack, 2019).

As Gilbert recounted on *The* ReLaunch *Podcast*:

> *I intuitively realized I did need stability, so I decided to go to Santa Monica for two weeks and just sit on the beach, taking time to stop and heal. My whole world was in a storage box. And, with that, I did start to feel better. I never had any desire to live in LA; in fact, I avoided it. But walking down the main street, I decided to stay. And, the very next day, I met Elizabeth Gilbert, author of the bestselling book Eat, Pray, Love, and we had this instant soul connection. She's sharing her book; I'm sharing my book. And then the following day, on the beach, I met my life partner. I was on a massive manifestation track, like a superhighway to transformation.*

Going full circle, Gilbert launched her own nonprofit to give back and support creative women in transition—an area she knows all too well (Goodreads, 2021; Tower 15 Productions, 2021). Having fallen to the bottom of the ladder, she always kept eyes forward and leveraged each rung on the ladder to reach the next, taking time to mindfully pause and reflect along the way. This is the 3HQ™ at work. The Heart, the Head, and the Higher Self in alignment, supporting Gilbert's journey to her best self at every step, ultimately embracing gratitude and supporting others in their journey.

QUESTIONS TO THINK ABOUT:

1. Have you ever decided to give up or start over? How did that decision affect your outcome?
2. Who are your role models, and why do you give them this honor? What do they have in common? What can you learn from them that applies to your life?
3. Write a letter to yourself as a child. What would you tell yourself? Now write a letter to yourself ten years in the future. How have you evolved toward your Higher Self? How will you evolve in the future? List specific goals. Keep these letters in a special place and reread them as reminders in the future.

CHAPTER FOURTEEN

EXPECT THE UNEXPECTED

One of my clients, "Meredith," epitomizes the unexpected way gratitude can enter via the back door and impact our lives when we least expect it, even in the midst of what could be the most unfortunate circumstances we might ever experience.

For most of her adult life, Meredith had been a successful home designer, flipping houses, building pools, remodeling bathrooms, and supporting her husband Ed's career as a top corporate executive in a massive energy company. Together, when she was in her fifties, they had reaped the benefits of his success and were enjoying close friendships with couples at the top of the company food chain. Ed's company was the kind of organization where the executives' wives were all best friends, their kids hung out and grew up together, and the couples socialized and vacationed together.

When the economy faltered around 2012, some of Meredith's clients—many of them friends and Ed's business associates—decided they couldn't pay Meredith's bills. She didn't press them. Times were tough, after all. She and Ed began using his investments to pay off her unpaid contractors so her workers could keep food on the table. Ultimately, they decided to close Meredith's business. Still, Ed's job seemed solid. His work and their life were inextricably intertwined. And Ed's career was more than a job—it was a lifestyle, encouraged by the firm to foster teamwork and success. The company was their "family." Or so they believed.

Then Ed had an unexpected health issue that necessitated emergency heart surgery. He nearly died on the table. "The hospital waiting room was filled with our friends from the company," said Meredith. Shortly after he returned to work, the company's chief executive officer held one of his regular weekend barbecues at his home. Twenty people, all part of their close-knit senior executive crowd, were there. It seemed like a typical get-together, everyone glad to see Ed back in action. Then, the following Tuesday, ninety days after he'd returned to work, and before his recovery was even complete, Ed was told his position had been eliminated. Meredith realized at least four people at the barbecue had known this was going to happen, but nobody had given her a clue. "They looked us straight in the eye," she said.

Gossip began burning up the grapevine, and it got back to Meredith—whose intuition was on fire too—that the word was Ed must have done something to deserve this. She began to feel sick.

Ed was in precarious health, their debts were mounting, and they had to put their house on the market. One day, in the midst of this, Meredith walked into a restaurant to find a number of the "group" having lunch. One of them was a woman, part of a couple to whom Meredith and Ed had loaned a hundred thousand dollars, who had been conspicuously out of touch. In fact, she realized, most of the "group" had been conspicuously out of touch.

"What's going on?" this woman asked Meredith, loudly enough that everyone in the restaurant, which was packed with the wives of her husbands' associates, could hear every word. "What's with the 'For Sale' sign outside your house? Why didn't you guys tell me your house was for sale?" A roomful of ice-cold eyes turned to Meredith.

"I was absolutely mortified," she said, still shaken. "It was soul-crushing. I decided right then, in the middle of the restaurant, to relinquish all my relationships with these people and walk away from them."

Meredith disconnected not just from her "friends," but from her emotions. For ten years, the memory of this scene brought chills and defined her life. It became the mother of all B.U.G.S.

"I went into roadblock mode," Meredith said. Finally, the couple moved to Santa Barbara and started a company from the ground up. Then they made a bad investment and lost everything once again. At that point, Ed had to have another heart bypass, which he barely survived.

"I no longer trusted what I had to say, and no one was there to listen. I knew in my heart, though, I needed to get my voice back," said Meredith.

She decided to take action and connected with The ReLaunch Co., where I worked closely with her on a ninety-day plan:

I threw myself into it. I realized no matter how affluent or broke you are, you can't compromise who you are. Things are just things. We get enjoyment out of giving material things to people, but much more than that is what gift you can give of yourself.

I want to look successful. We're conditioned for that, and it's very difficult to show vulnerability. I had to become an empty vessel, and now I'm filling it up with things that matter to me. I now have a lifestyle of success—on my own terms, as I define it—and I'm so grateful for it. My husband and I have a business that's starting to do well. We've doubled sales this year. I have a good balance between a healthy lifestyle and reflecting on what my limiting beliefs were, confronting them, and becoming much more in touch with myself with others.

I don't deny I like material things. But, on a way deeper level, I like the reward of helping other women who are in a stuck position, which I had been. And what's come out of it is now I'm giving back—working with young women who, for various reasons, are going through their own stuff. I'm teaching them design, and the group keeps growing. Through my voice, I'm providing love and receiving it back. So, it's not about things for me anymore. It's about people. About giving.

Meredith isn't stopping there. She's become a coach with my ReLaunch company and, using her design background, she's working on creating villages for homeless women. "After so many years, I have let go of my limiting beliefs," she says. "That has opened up so many doors."

From her vantage point as a former homeless woman, Cali Gilbert says:

> *Anything is possible. As humans, we don't really realize how powerful we are. It's almost as if we are afraid of our own power. So, we kind of hide it, or don't allow ourselves to shine. And that's so sad because each of us is unique in our own way. We've got these incredible gifts that we should be able to share with the world. Manifesting gratitude is about this amplification, this idea you're just turning up the volume of gratitude. And it's such an awesome state.*

Holocaust survivor, international best-selling author, and inspirational speaker Dr. Erica Miller has faced almost unimaginable challenges. She says life takes "courage, perseverance, and the ability to find gratitude in every situation"—a lesson she was forced to learn as a seven-year-old experiencing the horrors of living in a Nazi holding camp. Attributing her resilience and determination to the four years she spent imprisoned, she believes she is who she is today because, and in spite of, her experiences and adversities (as she said in *The* ReLaunch *Podcast*).

Surviving the Holocaust, launching a women's wear business, and surviving homelessness to walk the red carpet at the Oscars are hardly on the same plane, much less the same category. Yet they are all on the same planet, Planet Gratitude, sharing this basic human response. When I see a columbine blooming on a Colorado hike, I feel gratitude. It's microscopic compared to other motivations for gratitude, but the point is it's there and visible. I can mine it from the deepest well of my persona, and that in turn can create a subtle shift—for me and those around me who encounter my vibration.

When it comes to energy and the vibration it gives off, like attracts like. Smaller, more subtle levels of gratitude stimulate lower levels of energy vibrations, which attract similar levels of vibrations. It's like using poor quality fuel on a high-performance car. Eventually, you're looking at engine trouble.

But that doesn't mean you have to buy a new car, or that changes can't be made, or that without massive changes you completely drop off the cliff of the scale of attractions. A case is to be made for tune-ups. Even something as simple as a high five to the mirror or an "I love you" can start the ball rolling that makes a shift. A hug from a child. A smile. Even a well-made, delicious latte or tea. Sometimes—often—that's all we get. Sometimes—often—that's enough, and we need to remember that. The point is we are all on the gratitude spectrum. We can tap into it, and we can amplify it as we grow our dreams.

At the end of my mom's life, when we knew she was terminal and the clock was ticking, she and I decided that rather than focus on the inevitable sadness to come, we would flip that precious time on its head and commit to something special between us that could spark gratitude.

Finding the Light in Darkness

When I lived in Los Angeles, my mom was a travel agent, so she got deals on amazing trips. When she was single and I was in my early twenties, we would take advantage of some great deals and mother/daughter time. One special place was especially luxurious. We were reminded of it constantly when we flipped through magazines and saw gorgeous images of the Golden Door, a famous luxury spa and retreat. Mom was constantly trying to get me to go there with her, and we always had a reason it couldn't happen. We kept saying, "We've got to do this trip. We've got to do this trip." Any time is difficult, so of course it never happened. Then Mom got sick, and even as she weakened, she was wondering when we could take our trip. Before it became too late, I finally said, "Mom, let's just do it." We arranged for her to pause her treatment for a week, and we went to Golden Door.

Golden Door, 2019

It was a magical experience and everything we wanted, although of course we couldn't do many of the activities we'd always planned to do together. We couldn't go together for the 6 a.m. hikes every day, so I did them alone.

The second morning we were there, after I had gone on the hike, I knocked on Mom's door. She opened it in tears and said, "I think we might have waited too long. I just don't know if I can stay the week." With that, I brought in a spiritual "energy clearer" and lay next to my mom on the bed while the energy clearer worked on both of us, using mindfulness-based cognitive and energy healing tools.

This woman looked right at my mom and said, "I know how much you love your daughter. I know how much you love helping her and listening to all the things she does with her work, but you're going to be more useful for her on the other side." And that one comment gave my mom such peace that she ended up feeling better and was able to stay the rest of the trip.

Mom was able to do a few little things during the week. As it turned out, a famous actress was there and she and my mom became friends. They would sit for hours at lunch, and I'd join them, then get up and do an activity. Although Mom couldn't do that, she could—and did—sit and talk to this famous woman. Mom developed deep friendships, real connections with every single person in the group. They had pictures taken, and the smiles on every one of those faces was gratitude incarnate. When we left, everybody wanted to continue to follow her journey. It ended up being such a special time for both of us.

I was so grateful this incredible event happened. Yes, I waited too long. But, in retrospect, maybe that *was* the right time, the exact right time, the time when my mom—and I—needed it the most. We had pierced the veil of the superficial and were operating at a deep, inner 3HQ™ level, bringing what was inside forward at an energy level that, while it may seem low due to the circumstances, was in this case simply radiant, like embers glowing in the night.

Although my mom had been living from her Heart to her Head to her Higher Self almost every day of her life, I noticed an incredible shift in the way she was showing up and moving forward. She seemed to be operating on an even higher level, in absolute peace, taking steps forward with positive internal thoughts, a lifted Heart, an open mind, and showing up in the pure, protective cloak of her Highest Self. She illustrated the 3HQ™ effect in living action—the giving off of positive energy to others that results in a circular return of energy, reinforcing inner peace and joy (Young, 2020).

Our trip together evolved from "going to a spa" to a spiritual connection, a condition we both embraced. The physical activities could no longer be shared, but the bigger gift of gratitude remains long after the trip itself. These things are fun, of course—who doesn't appreciate a great facial?—but they seem so superficial compared to what we shared

and the gratitude overflowing inside me because I had these last moments with her. I can't forget how grateful my mom was for that week and how grateful I and the wonderful people she met on the trip remain for the shared experience. This gratitude is forever imprinted on our lives.

We can recognize so many everyday opportunities, but we overlook them because we take them for granted. They are just *right there in your face*, totally visible, but we push back and make them invisible. When Mom and I left the retreat, I realized this and started to see things differently, to appreciate more of what I have in my life now. I still follow this path; it was a key part in my life-changing move from California to Colorado.

After being physically invisible for so many months in an apartment, Erich and I knew we needed more of the earth—hikes, skies, taking in the beauty—a higher-level energy from within that needed to be physically brought to the surface. Enter the 3HQ™. All the "buts" and "shoulds" fell away. I packed up two decades-plus of California life and we moved to Boulder. It didn't take long to see the result. As I walked my first hike and looked at the view, a huge smile seemed to take over my entire being. *Visible gratitude.*

For me, it all started with writing in my journal. It's fascinating that gratitude writing, including but not limited to journaling, has a scientifically measurable positive impact on feelings of well-being and happiness within one to three months (Wong et al., 2018). I guess I was right on schedule.

Even if you ultimately get that dream job, that dream man, don't wait until you have that whatever, because even if it does happen, you've missed so much along the way. My lesson was you don't have to wait until someone you love is dying or you're dying to touch other people or start doing what's on the bucket list and accumulate things that spark—and return—gratitude. We can start doing that now, just by noticing, by incorporating that daily visible gratitude into our lives.

That's the power you manifest when the Invisible becomes Visible Gratitude. It is the power that the triple threat of the 3HQ™—the Heart, the Head, and the Higher Self—can bring to your life.

Are you ready to open the jar and release the fireflies? If so, what if you and a partner were to create a Thirty Day Gratitude Challenge Team? You might focus on a Month of Gratitude. Even a Seven Day Challenge might be a starting point. You can choose a thought, a word, or even a picture to express gratitude and share. The two of you will be partners in creating a Circle of Gratitude. Since it takes sixty-two to sixty-seven days to create a new belief, you will be well on your way after thirty days to creating a personal gratitude practice. Then, start another month. The circle continues and grows. The beauty of this is you can tailor your approach to whatever aspect of your life that you choose: family, work, friendship, or romance. You are expanding your 3HQ™ to bring gratitude into your life, and that of

others. When you do that on a regular, habit-forming basis, you build a resilient platform to manifest your desires and dreams. Customize as you choose; you are curating a life to fit and empower your best future. You've never had a better time to give yourself the gift of *you*.

Looking into the future, it's exciting to think of all of us participating in a Gratitude Community, sharing and putting this message out to as many people as possible. Because if we can have these graceful leaders—with values built on the power, strength, wisdom, and higher essence of our 3HQ™—imagine where we'll be.

It's about the Heart, the Head, and the Higher Self and the fact that, when they work in alignment, all three play a role that combines to act as an accelerator to achieving your goals. The Heart is all about emotional strength, and the Head is a power source. We know knowledge is power. Leveraging them together sharpens the ability to hear your intuition talking to you and to listen to it. That's how you get to your Higher Self. It's an infinity of three circles because life constantly happens, with no real beginning or end.

I have come to realize this spiritually oriented trilogy is a distillation of the essence of my mom, the woman who had lived it and instilled it within me. A woman who didn't have much longer to be alive who showed me how to live. It's truly amazing how even the most challenging transitions can lead you through change to triumph.

These breakthroughs and solutions come from bringing what is invisible to the visible surface. Solutions are fueled via the Higher Self where, if we permit it, universal connections open the portal to the vast, hidden resources of our inner, untapped consciousness. This is where we break down our personal barriers to get where we want to be.

It's when we understand how to live guided by insight into our 3HQ™ that a purposeful and meaningful ReLaunch journey can begin. Then we don't just live; we can transform. By igniting our lives with the 3HQ™ Method, sparks begin to fly. Each of us has the tools to connect from a place of truth originating deep inside, a catalyst that allows us to fulfill our mission in the most aligned and authentic way.

From this basis of authenticity, we gain the clarity that allows us to see solutions, opportunities, and gifts that may have been masked or blurred by clutter and distortion. In this way, it makes all the sense in the world that I close this conversation with a flashback to my mom, the master of the ReLaunch Flip.

Click! It is well into Mom's last days. No treatment is coming to the rescue, and we both know it. We focus instead on spending time together, having some of the best talks of our lives, delving deeply into many of the things that will become the basis of my future business,

relationships, and this book. Each of us is headed to her next transformation. Mom told it like it is: "Oh, Hilary. It's *so good*."

QUESTIONS TO THINK ABOUT:

1. The virtual world is a fact of life. How can you practice gratitude virtually on a consistent basis? Can you think of three ways you could add this key value to your virtual lifestyle to add a gratitude practice to your technology tools?
2. "Overlooked gratitude opportunities" are like diamonds cast into a field. Can you identify and harvest some of your overlooked chances to show gratitude just in this day alone?

3. Who do you consider to be your community or tribe? What are their values? How can you mutually support yourselves on a daily basis through gratitude?

THE RELAUNCH WORKSPACE

THE 3HQ™

Energy Levels (Vibration)
Purpose
G-Zone (Growth, Greatness, Gratitude)

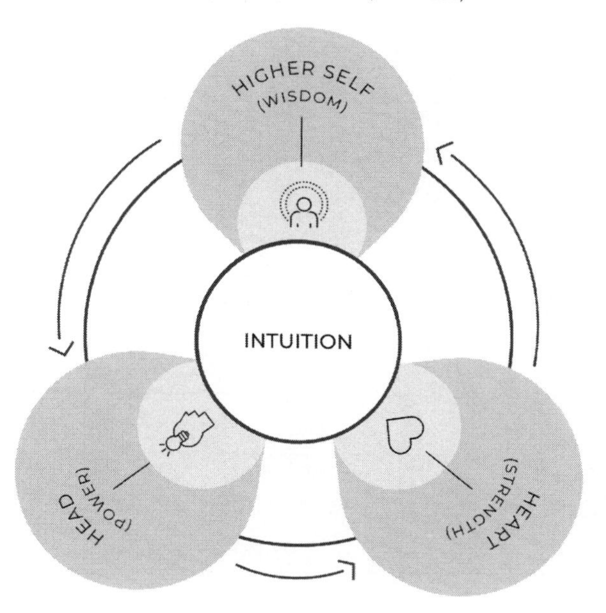

Tune-in Thoughts ←—(B.U.G.S.)—→ Emotional Blocks / Trauma
ReLaunch Flip™ Self Like > Self Love
Identity Your Why

RELAUNCH WORKSPACE

Today's Date: ________

RELAUNCH WORKSPACE

Today's Date: ________

RELAUNCH WORKSPACE

Today's Date: __________

RELAUNCH WORKSPACE

Today's Date: ________

QUESTIONS TO THINK ABOUT:

1. When you review the 3HQ™ diagram, where do you feel your strengths are, and what will you start working toward today to live a 3HQ™ lifestyle?
2. Who are your role models, and why do you give them this honor? What do they have in common? What can you learn from them that applies to your life?
3. Write a letter to yourself from your future self who is living in the identity of 3HQ™. How does it feel? How are you showing up daily? What is manifesting in your life?

Are you or your business ReLaunch-Ready? Visit our community at The ReLaunch Co. using this QR code so you can manifest your best lifestyle of success and gratitude.

POSTSCRIPT

WHAT'S NEXT?

By Hilary DeCesare

Hi there. It's me again. You thought this book was over? You know what, so did I! But then I reread it myself again—and again. Each time, as I hope you did, I found a fresh angle that inspired me, made me think, and fired up my 3HQ™. I think so many of us have a story already inside, but haven't figured out the key to unlocking its power and bringing its magic—the magic of you—to the surface. When we finally figure out how to get there, how to connect our head with our heart and then ignite it all with our higher self, or take even a few steps in that direction, the inertia just cracks wide open. Almost as if we've been constrained in a shell that suddenly falls away. When we align our 3HQ™, we break out into a new phase of possibilities. That is some amazing achievement.

For me, that process led to this book. Which, in turn, led me to you and, I hope, a relationship where we're kindred souls on a road to even further and greater discovery—about ourselves, our relationships, our work, our families, and what we can achieve—now that we have the toolbox open and the tools in our hands.

After a recent trip to Italy, I began to wonder how Michelangelo felt when he first started seeing those human forms emerge from the marble. With his heart, his talent, and his tools, he created something from those blocks of marble that would become some of the most exquisite artworks on earth. The idea alone was simple, a statue of a person. There are plenty of beautiful sculptures, but his work was singular in its adept portrayal of humanity. It wasn't just in the execution of the idea; it was in the heart of the artist which shone through the stone. To me it felt like, in a similar way, we are each creating the greatest singular creations—ourselves.

As I sat with the completed pages of my book, my own special creation, I remembered how I had once thought it would be impossible to write, much less publish. Closing my eyes, I imagined myself twenty years ago in Silicon Valley. Racing to meetings, catching flights, seeing my kids on the fly, marriage on the rocks. I barely had space in my life to sleep, much less dream. Yet, dream I did—as do you, or you would not have read this book. Somewhere, deep inside, the spark was not extinguished. By reconnecting with myself, I learned how to surface my authentic self and be me. And I am a woman. I am named Hilary. I am the mother of five fabulous children, a wife to an incredible man, and an author.

It's hard even now for me to realize this isn't a dream. I open my eyes and look at the cover. When you write a book, there is always a cover of some sort. This one, a match igniting the glittering sparkler of a heart, leapt out at me from hundreds of images. The picture said it all for me. Spark your heart to ignite your life. For me, this book is proof that it can be done.

So now what?

Are we greedy to want more? Am I ungrateful to be thinking, What's the new next? Let's think about this. What's probably the oldest process in existence? Evolution. Evolution is the essence of life. Evolution is the essence of ReLaunch. It's a concept that's buried deep inside us because it's born of our DNA. What doesn't evolve ceases to exist. Those who evolve not only survive but sustain and grow. We're all in this evolution thing together, along with everything else in existence. And so, we seek the next level, and then the next, of our personal evolution. Each level consists of a ReLaunch all its own. The spark may vary, but the process is constant.

We've all been in a whirlpool, a triple-threat ReLaunch swirling around us—global, professional, and personal. On some level or another, we've all been affected. It's inescapable. Maybe your relationship has been impacted. Maybe your children. Perhaps, like me, you've lost a parent—or two. Or your job has shifted, your household impacted. These are all

ReLaunch situations. But we have the tools. We can summon our own spark to rekindle our 3HQ™ and take control of these ReLaunches.

The question of Now what? will always be there—as long as there is a "next." And maybe it's not necessary to know the answers up front. Goals are important, but to get there you can take innumerable paths—and all can be accessed through the 3HQ™ Method. I never imagined that the sadness and tears of my mother's death would lead me to this book, let alone and the joy and opportunities it has brought me. She gave me the gift of the ReLaunch Flip that made a perspective shift possible, and it's the gift that keeps relaunching itself.

One thing that makes moving on and creating a "new next" tough is the prospect of buyer's remorse. If you've ever had a breakup, a divorce, or suddenly think your dream job is a lemon, that's buyer's remorse. The 3HQ™ Method is based on authenticity, so if you activate your 3HQ™, you have a pretty good chance of deciding based on your authentic self and desires. But there are always circumstances that shift under your feet. For example, working from home sounded great. But suddenly you find you miss the office routine, your tribe and connections, even the relative peace of the commute on the train or that time alone with your thoughts in the car. You feel disconnected by this new, unfamiliar experience. You're not who you were anymore. Even the plant you brought home from the office, which thrived somehow under fluorescent light, drooped and died in your kitchen window. The printer died, too, and you can't fix it, and there's nobody to come repair it. What happened to the dream? Maybe it wasn't the dream?

Here's where you loop back, open your toolbox, relight the spark, and revisit the 3HQ™ Method. Dig deep and ask yourself, not just what is wrong, but what is right. Flip the script. You make your own routine. If you have Zoom calls, you can go barefoot to meetings. You have new, different opportunities—without wheels—for alone time. You can join a book club finally with the time you save on the commute. Making a flip list is a great first step, a way to get started on your new next.

But maybe something is stopping you from taking that new next step. I know that when it came to starting this book, I hesitated more than once. Maybe it was page one trauma—staring at that empty page and thinking of a couple hundred more to go. Maybe I was better off sticking with my "same old" than putting myself out there? Then my own fear of failing would be extinguished. Finally, I figured out the cure, the step that would eventually close the gap between wanting and doing. I wrote page one—though the first page of this book is not that same page one. Getting to the first page of this book took many versions and rearrangements of it. But page one led to page one. And then page two. Find your page one just by starting.

Starting is evolving. Nothing happens without a beginning. If you ever wonder about getting started, retrieve your copy of this book from the shelf, bedside table, or the friend you lent it to and open it to page one. Reread the book. Rinse and repeat. Go for it.

Now, back to buyer's remorse. Apparently, it's so common that it has a new name, "the great regret" (Stillman, n.d.).

For instance, quitting a job can cause emotional backlash. According to a USA Today poll, just one in five job switchers like their new job enough to stay (Davidson, 2022). Shocker, a substantial percentage stated they made the move for money. What's wrong with this picture? They were likely unable to get out of their heads and into their hearts. Sensitive to this, companies are responding with "retention bonuses" (Stillman, n.d.). Fighting fire with fire? Here's a message for both team members and management—How about fighting fire with sparks? Sparks from, and to, the heart. Leading with the heart when tough decisions are staring you in the face is a great action step to take when choices come your way.

This is especially true for solopreneurs, mompreneurs, and the new purposepreneurs, along with those of us who work from home, cyberspace, or any place pretty much on our own.

One of the great things about our heart is that no matter how often we lose it, give it away, or break it, it remains firmly attached to us for life. It is life, waiting and ready for the call to action. Sometimes working, or just being on your own, can feel disconnected and lonely—but you can feel lonely and even alienated in a crowd, cubicle, shared space, huge corner office, or tree house. Your social situation isn't about your surroundings, it's about you. Here again, tapping into your 3HQ™ can be your shelter, even temporarily. It can be a kind of transitory luxury of time to access your higher sense of purpose and self—your inner core. I like to think of it like glamping. Those glamorous tent camps you see in ads for bare basics resorts that feature six hundred thread-count sheets and comfy rugs casually tossed over a sand dune for a picnic in the wild. The place to stop over when you're not ready to commit, but meanwhile you don't want to be deprived. Your 3HQ™ is like a travel insurance policy—no matter what you decide, you're going to get full value.

We have an incredible advantage over Michelangelo when creating our masterpiece, our new next. Once Michelangelo chiseled into that block of marble, there was no turning back. But instead of marble we work with clay. Remodeling is not only permitted but encouraged in ReLaunching. Sculpt away. You're evolving into the new next you, and it's going to be epic.

Change is always somewhat scary. That's why I call my longest-reach goals "scazy," a combination of scary and crazy. Yes! I invented a word. With one word, you can begin any change. You can begin any page. You can begin… a book.

Or you can end it.

Go for your new next. And let it be scazy.

XoXo, Hilary

ACKNOWLEDGMENTS

Does everything have a silver lining? I believe so, as this book would not have been written without my mom's passing. I continue to explore my own 3HQ™ while inspired by my mom as well as the incredible journeys of so many fellow ReLaunchers.

A heartfelt thank you to my family—Dad, Inge, Greg, my amazing kids Derek, Dani, and Rosie, and stepchildren Will and Henry—for believing in me, letting me their share stories, and the messages along the way. Liani and Mic, thank you for a united family through all the ReLaunches. Don Xavier and Mandi Vargas, my soul family, thank you for waking me up to the invisible and visible in such a profound way.

To Rebecca Hall-Gruyter, who believed I had a story to tell and published *Step into Your Brilliant Purpose,* which allowed me to become a best-selling author. It led me to a much bigger story to share. Eric Koester, founder of Creator Institute—thank you for pushing me to get that book out of my head and learn to actually write a book. New Degree Press team—Bianca daSilva, John Saunders, and the massive team behind me—thank you for thinking the book was publishable and keeping me committed to the journey.

A special appreciation is due to my incredible mentors, Jim Fortin, John Assaraf, John Gray, and Dr. Shannon Irvine, for pushing me to challenge my own thinking.

To the ReLaunch Team, thank you for holding down the fort when I went into my cave for writing. I am so grateful to have each of you creating Global ReLaunches. Liz Nickles, you are a brilliant creative and your help and friendship over the past ten-plus years have been invaluable.

To the amazing Indiegogo donators who stepped up with their support in the early days

—I was overwhelmed by the support. Thank all of you for your belief in what I had to share:

Alison Shunneson, Angela Butler, Anne Abreu, Audrey Hall, Belinda Smith, Brianna Ricks, Casey Howard, Cathy Caldwell, Christina Samuelson, Danita Wilcox, Dolf and Sue Kahle, Dr. Jackie Buettner, Dr. Timothy and Inge Howard, Eric Koester, Greg Howard, Holly Haket, Janet Smith-Tolale, Jennifer and Steve Sengelmann, Jennifer Callahan, Jennifer Lee Miramontes, Jennifer Takagi, Jeri Cohen, John DeCesare, Judith L. Trezza, Katelyn Brown, Kathleen Foutz, Kelley Brenninger, Kelly Foster, Kelly Lee, Kim Bruce, Kimberly Pressman, Kori O'brien, Kristina Yarrington, Leslie Karren, Liani Kotcher, Louelle Chimes, Maury and Leslie

Blackman, Megan Fitzgerald, Megan Fitzgerald, Michael DeCesare, Michale Gabriel, Michelle Abraham, Michelle Woodward. Monique Londeree, Nancy George, Nancy Tiano, Nicole Cattan, Paige McCullough, Pamela Bergren, Rebecca Simmons, Rich Bernstein, Robert DeChellis, Rose Viggiano, Sally Raccuglia, Shanon Wagner, Shona Gupta, Stacy Straub, Stefanie Bryning, Susan Douglas, Tamir and Roberta Keshen, Tara Cooper, Taylor Tompkins, Timothy J. Taylor, Tracy C. Letzerich, Valerie Shepherd, Vicky Karcich, Wendy McGee.

To those who are going through the most significant ReLaunches of their lives—Tamir Keshin and Iris Horowitz—you inspire me to live life today and to be grateful for the love of great friends and family.

Finally, I want to thank my husband Erich for believing in my dreams and making them ours. Never have I felt more loved, and never have I wanted to give so much love. It's just forever!

And to all the ReLaunchers out there who are now mastering the 3HQ™ Method, I want to give you Erich's panini recipe to treat yourself or to make for someone else. Enjoy!

Ingredients

- 2 slices of Ciabatta
- 1 Zucchini
- 1 Onion
- 1 Bell Pepper
- 1 ounce of Sun-Dried Tomatoes
- 2 tbsp Sour Cream
- 4 tbsp Mayo
- 1/2 cup Mozzarella
- Chives
- Parsley
- Salt
- Pepper
- 1 tsp Garlic
- Powder
- 1 tsp Italian
- Seasoning
- Olive Oil

Prep:

- Slice zucchini crosswise into thick rounds.
- Dice 1/2 of the onion.
- Mince parsley and chives.
- Halve ciabatta.
- Finely chop sun-dried tomatoes.

Cook Zucchini & Onion

- Mix zucchini and diced onion with a drizzle of olive oil, 1/2 tsp of garlic powder, 1/2 tsp italian seasoning, salt and pepper.
- Heat a drizzle of oil in a large pan over medium-high heat.
- Cook Vegetables until golden brown.
- Transfer vegetables to a plate.

Char Bell Pepper

- Char the bell pepper over a gas stove using kitchen tongs.
- Let cool, peel and slice.

The Secret Sauce:

- Combine 4 tbsp mayo, 2 tbsp sour cream, parsley, chives and 1/2 tsp garlic powder.
- Season with salt and pepper.

Final Assembly

- Spread sauce onto ciabattas. • Fill ciabatas with mozzarella, sun-dried tomatoes, onion, bell pepper and zucchini. • Heat a drizzle of oil in a pan. • Once hot, add sandwiches. Press with a spatula.
- Cook until bread is toasted and cheese melts. • Transfer paninis to a plate and serve.

APPENDIX

PREFACE:

Bennett, Kevin. "Why Do We Only Use 10 Percent of the Brain? Despite Evidence, We Do Not Seem Comfortable Letting Go of This Neuromyth." *Psychology Today* (blog), March 28, 2018. https://www.psychologytoday.com/us/blog/modern-minds/201803/why-do-we-only-use-10-percent-the-brain.

Bradberry, Travis. "Are You Emotionally Intelligent? Here's How to Know for Sure: Emotional Intelligence Is a Huge Driver of Success." *Inc.*, March 24, 2015. https://www.inc.com/travis-bradberry/are-you-emotionally-intelligent-here-s-how-to-know-for-sure.html.

Del Cul, Antoine, Sylvain Baillet, and Stanislas Dehaene. "Brain Dynamics Underlying the Nonlinear Threshold for Access to Consciousness." *PLoS Biology* 5, no. 10 (October 2007): e260. https://www.ncbi.nlm.nih.gov/pmc/articles/PMC1988856/.

McGreal, Scott A. "The Illusory Theory of Multiple Intelligences." *Psychology Today* (blog), November 23, 2013. https://www.psychologytoday.com/us/blog/unique-everybody-else/201311/the-illusory-theory-multiple-intelligences.

Oppland, Mike. “How Psychology Combats False and Self-Limiting Beliefs.” *PositivePsychology*, June 12, 2021. https://positivepsychology.com/false-beliefs/.

Wiest, Brianna. “13 Ways to Start Training Your Subconscious Mind to Get What You Want.” *Forbes*, September 12, 2018. https://www.forbes.com/sites/briannawiest/2018/09/12/13-ways-to-start-training-your-subconscious-mind-to-get-what-you-want/?sh=5c6d8517d69f.

INTRODUCTION:

Antanaityte, Neringa. “Mind Matters: How to Effortlessly Have More Positive Thoughts.” TLEX Institute, November 15, 2021. https://tlexinstitute.com/how-to-effortlessly-have-more-positive-thoughts/.

Brooks, Arthur C. “The Clocklike Regularity of Major Life Changes.” *The Atlantic*, September 10, 2020. https://www.theatlantic.com/family/archive/2020/09/major-life-changes-happen-clocklike-regularity/616243/.

Cook, Ian. “Who Is Driving the Great Resignation?” *Harvard Business Review*, September 15, 2021. https://hbr.org/2021/09/who-is-driving-the-great-resignation.

Fox, Michelle. “Women Are Leading the Way in the ‘Great Resignation’: Here’s What It Means for Employers and Job Seekers.” *CNBC*, November 17, 2021. https://www.cnbc.com/2021/11/17/women-are-quitting-at-higher-rates-than-men-during-the-great-resignation.html.

Lang, Susan S. "Crisis or Just Stress? Cornell Researcher Finds the Midlife Crisis is Less Common Than Many Believe." *Cornell Chronicle*, March 19, 2001. https://news.cornell.edu/stories/2001/03/midlife-crisis-less-common-many-believe.

Lau, Yolanda. "Increasing Mindfulness in The Workplace." *Forbes*, October 5, 2020. https://www.forbes.com/sites/forbeshumanresourcescouncil/2020/10/05/increasing-mindfulness-in-the-workplace/?sh=6f452f756956.

Morin, Amy. "What Are the Signs of a Midlife Crisis? Midlife Can Be the Unhappiest Time in a Person's Life." Verywell Mind, November 05, 2021. https://www.verywellmind.com/what-are-the-signs-of-a-midlife-crisis-4175827.

World Bank. "World Development Indicators." Accessed September 16, 2021. https://databank.worldbank.org/source/world-development-indicators.

Chapter One:

Associated Press. "Facebook, WhatsApp, Instagram Suffer Worldwide Outage." *NPR*, updated October 4, 2021. https://www.npr.org/2021/10/04/1043098635/facebook-whatsapp-instagram-outage.

Bianchi, Nicole. *Small Brave Moves*. Potomac, MD: New Degree Press, 2021.

DeCesare, Hilary, and Kelly Ruta. "Episode 66: How to Build a Better and Stronger Version of Yourself." Produced by The ReLaunch Co. *The Silver Lined* ReLaunch. July 14, 2021. Podcast, MP3 audio, 38:25. https://therelaunchco.com/podcast- episode-66-how-to-build-a-better-and-stronger-version-of-yourself-with-kelly-ruta/.

DeCesare, Hilary, and Jim Fortin. "Episode 9: You Are Never Stuck." Produced by The ReLaunch Co. *The Silver Lined* ReLaunch. October 6, 2021. Podcast, MP3 audio, 6:56. https://therelaunchco.com/podcast-episode-9-you-are-never-stuck/.

Smith, Raven. "On Surviving the Great Facebook Blackout of 2021." *Vogue*, October 6, 2021. https://www.vogue.com/article/on-surviving-the-great-facebook-blackout-of-2021.

Stevenson, Ross. "Disconnection in a Connected World: An insight to Our Relationship with Technology and Each Other." Thrive Global, October 22, 2018. https://thriveglobal.com/stories/disconnection-in-a-connected-world-2/.Oprah.com. "What to Do If You've Lost Your Sense of Purpose." Accessed August 15, 2021. https://www.oprah.com/inspiration/how-to-find-your-sense-of-purpose-again_1.

CHAPTER TWO:

Bellevue Christian Counseling. "Childhood Trauma Effects that Often Surface Later in Life." January 7, 2016. https://bellevuechristiancounseling.com/articles/childhood-trauma-effects-that-often-surface-later-in-life.

DeCesare, Hilary, and Britt Frank. "Episode 69: How the Brain and the Body Work Together with Britt Frank." Produced by The ReLaunch Co. *The Silver Lined* ReLaunch. April 8, 2021. Podcast, MP3 audio, 13:08. https://therelaunchco.com/podcast-episode-69-how-the-brain-and-the-body-work-together-with-britt-frank/.

DeCesare, Hilary, and Rose Bond. "Episode 41: Why Reclaiming Your Life Starts with Thoughts and Beliefs with Star Rose Bond." Produced by The ReLaunch Co. *The Silver Lined* ReLaunch. January 1, 2021. Podcast, MP3 audio, 25:35. https://therelaunchco.com/podcast-episode-41-why-reclaiming-your-life-starts-with-thoughts-and-beliefs-with-star- rose-bond/.

Eating Disorder Hope (blog). "The Illusion of Control in the Development of Eating Disorders." Accessed November 15, 2021. https://www.eatingdisorderhope.com/blog/illusion-control-development-eating-disorders.

Eng, Monica. "How a High-Powered Lawyer Became a TikTok Superstar: Meet the Korean Vegan." *Washington Post*, October 4, 2021. https://www.washingtonpost.com/food/2021/10/04/korean-vegan-joanne-molinaro/.

Houry, Debra. "Identifying, Preventing, and Treating Childhood Trauma." Centers for Disease Control and Prevention, July 11, 2019. https://www.cdc.gov/washington/testimony/2019/t20190711.htm.

Mitchell, Elizabeth. "The Truth About Princess Diana's Struggle with Bulimia." The List.com, December 1, 2020. https://www.thelist.com/286907/the-truth-about-princess-dianas-struggle-with-bulimia/?utm_campaign=clip.

MindWise Innovations (blog). “The Impact of Trauma for Americans.” Accessed November 8, 2021. https://www.mindwise.org/blog/college/the-impact-of-trauma-for-americans/.

Molinaro, Joanne Lee. *The Korean Vegan Cookbook: Reflections and Recipes from Omma’s Kitchen*. New York: Avery, 2021.

PACER’s National Bullying Prevention Center. “Rates of Incidence.” Last updated November 2020. https://www.pacer.org/bullying/info/stats.asp.

Safronova, Valeriya. “Feeling Anxious? Journaling Might Help.” *New York Times*, October 7, 2021. https://www.nytimes.com/2021/10/07/style/therapy-notebooks-anxiety-depression-mindfulness.html.

Smith, Sally Bedell. “Diana in Search of Herself: Portrait of a Troubled Princess.” *New York Times*, accessed December 12, 2021. https://archive.nytimes.com/www.nytimes.com/books/first/s/smith-diana.html? scp=80&sq=royalpercent2520marriage&st=cse.

The Korean Vegan. “Meet Joanne Lee Molinaro.” Accessed November 20, 2021. https://thekoreanvegan.com/about.

Tzani, Calli. “Childhood Bullying Can Cause Lifelong Psychological Damage – Here’s How to Spot the Signs and Move On.” The Conversation, August 8, 2018. https://theconversation.com/.

Chapter Three:

Couric, Katie. *Going There*. New York: Little, Brown, 2021.

Gray, John. *Men Are from Mars, Women Are from Venus*. New York: HarperCollins, 2021.

Howes, Lewis. "You Don't Need to Be Perfect." *Entrepreneur*, May 8, 2017.
https://www.entrepreneur.com/article/293839. Lile, Samantha Pratt. "How These 3 Women Made It Into C-Suite." Beautiful.ai (blog), September 23, 2021.

https://www.beautiful.ai/blog/how-these-3-women-made-it-into-c-suite.

Mzumara, Maggie. "Impostor Syndrome Hurts High-Achieving Women." *Sunday Mail*, August 9, 2020.
https://www.sundaymail.co.zw/impostor-syndrome-hurts-high-achieving-women.

Tulshyan, Ruchika, and Jodi-Ann Burey. "Stop Telling Women They Have Imposter Syndrome." *Harvard Business Review*, February 11, 2021.
https://hbr.org/2021/02/stop-telling-women-they-have-imposter-syndrome.

Chapter Four:

Earle, Dana. "Retraining Your Brain: How Physical Therapists Use Neuroplasticity to Help Patients Overcome Brain Injuries." PT For Life, accessed November 20, 2021.
https://ptsmc.com/physical-therapy-neuroplasticity.

Evercoach. "Master the Hidden Rules of Creation to Access Unlimited Abundance & Achieve Unbelievable Results for Your Clients." Accessed November 26, 2021. https://www.evercoach.com/spiritual-life-coaching/special/ads.

Gladwell, Malcolm. *Outliers: The Story of Success*. New York: Little, Brown and Company, 2008.

Goewey, Don Joseph. "85 Percent of What We Worry About Never Happens." *HuffPost*, August 25, 2015. https://www.huffpost.com/entry/85-of-what-we-worry-about_b_8028368.

Goldhill, Olivia. "Turns Out It Doesn't Take 10,000 Hours to Become an Expert." *Quartz*, September 8, 2019. https://qz.com/1705070/the-10000-hour-rule-has-been-disproven-now-what/.

Karimi, Faith. "Why Olympic Figure Skaters Don't Get Dizzy." CNN, February 16, 2022. https://www.cnn.com/2022/02/16/sport/olympics-figure-skating-questions-cec/index.html.

Kelly, John D. "Law of the Echo: Negative Feelings Are Attracted to Negative Events." Healio, April 2, 2013. https://www.healio.com/news/orthopedics/20200408/law-of-the-echo-negative-feelings-are-attracted-to-negative-events.

Lester, David, Judith Hvezda, Shannon Sullivan, and Roger Plourde. "Maslow's Hierarchy of Needs and Psychological Health." *Journal of General Psychology* 109, no. 1 (July 1983): 83–85. https://pubmed.ncbi.nlm.nih.gov/28150561/.

Morin, Amy. "This Is How Your Thoughts Become Your Reality." *Forbes*, June 15, 2016. https://www.forbes.com/sites/amymorin/2016/06/15/this-is-how-your-thoughts-become-your-reality/?sh=6cd49009528a.

Park, Denise C., and Chih-Mao Huang. "Culture Wires the Brain: A Cognitive Neuroscience Perspective." *Perspectives on Psychological Science* 5, no. 4 (July 2010): 391–400. https://www.ncbi.nlm.nih.gov/pmc/articles/PMC3409833/.

Wickman, Forrest. "The Beatles Say Goodbye to Hamburg." *Vox*, December 17, 2012. https://slate.com/culture/2012/12/the-beatles-live-in-hamburg-50-years-ago-the-beatles-played-their-final-shows-at-the-star-club-at-germany-audio.html.

Williams, Rachelle. "What Is Fear? And How to Use It as Motivation." Chopra.com, November 9, 2018. https://chopra.com/articles/what-is-fear-and-how-to-use-it-as-motivation.

Young, Emma. "Lifting the Lid on the Unconscious." *NewScientist*, July 25, 2018. https://www.newscientist.com/article/mg23931880-400-lifting-the-lid-on-the-unconscious/.

CHAPTER FIVE:

Amen, Daniel. "How Negative Thoughts Affect Brain Health + What to Do About Them." MBGMindfulness, October 17, 2019. https://www.mindbodygreen.com/articles/how-negative-thoughts-affect-brain-health-what-to-do-about-them.

Barrett, Lisa Feldman. “People’s Words and Actions Can Actually Shape Your Brain: A Neuroscientist Explains How.” Ideas.TED.Com, November 17, 2020. https://ideas.ted.com/peoples-words-and-actions-can-actually-shape-your-brain-a-neuroscientist-explains-how/.

Bianchi, Nicole. *Small Brave Moves*. Potomac, MD: New Degree Press, 2021.

DeCesare, Hilary, and John Assaraf. “Episode 80: How Your Beliefs Impact Your Behavior.” Produced by The ReLaunch Co. *The Silver Lined* ReLaunch. September 9, 2020. Podcast, MP3 audio, 38:27. https://therelaunchco.com/podcast-episode- 80-how-your-beliefs-impact-your-behavior-with-john-assaraf/.

Godoy, Maria. “Instead of New Year’s Resolutions, Start and Stick with ‘Tiny Habits.’” NPR: Life Kit, December 28, 2021. https://www.npr.org/2020/02/25/809256398/tiny-habits-are-the-key-to-behavioral-change.

Psychology Today (blog). “Repression.” Accessed November 22, 2021. https://www.psychologytoday.com/us/basics/repression.

Talk of the Nation. “Can Thoughts and Action Change Our Brains?” NPR, February 2, 2007. https://www.npr.org/templates/story/story.php?storyId=7131130.

Torre, Vanessa. “Is ‘Powering Through’ Really a Good Thing? Or Are We Doing More Harm Than Good?” Medium, February 16, 2019. https://vanessatorre.medium.com/is-powering-through-really-a-good-thing-d4726f07b442.

CHAPTER SIX:

DeCesare, Hilary, and Melissa Bird. "Episode 34: How to Trust Yourself and Your Village with Dr. Melissa Bird." Produced by The ReLaunch Co. *The Silver Lined* ReLaunch. October 29, 2020. Podcast, MP3 audio, 42:49. https://therelaunchco.com/podcast-episode-34-how-to-trust-yourself-and-your-village-dr-melissa-bird/.

Ruef-Lindquist, Sarah. "Retirement Planning for Women: Understanding the 'Bag Lady' Syndrome." Allen Insurance and Financial, March 31, 2021. https://allenif.com/bag-lady-syndrome/.

Seegert, Liz. "Bag Lady Syndrome: The Fear of Dying Broke and Alone." Silver Century Foundation, March 27, 2017. https://www.silvercentury.org/2017/03/losing-sleep-for-fear-of-becoming-a-bag-lady/.

Tisdale, Stacey. "Feminist Icon, Gloria Steinem, Shares Her Most Intimate Money Lessons with Wealth Wednesday's Stacey Tisdale." Mind Money Media, March 2, 2021. https://mindmoneymedia.com/stories/gloria-steinem-quotes-an-interview-with-gloria-steinem-about-her-relationship-with-money/.

Toller, Carol. "What Do Oprah, Gloria Steinem and Katie Couric Have in Common? They're All Terrified of Becoming Penniless." *Chatelaine*, April 16, 2007. https://www.chatelaine.com/living/budgeting/bag-lady-baggage/.

Ward, Kim. "Out-Smart Self-Sabotage: 5 Steps to Change Subconscious Beliefs." MBGMindfulness, October 29, 2020. https://www.mindbodygreen.com/0-11928/outsmart-selfsabotage-5-steps-to-change-subconscious-beliefs.html.

CHAPTER SEVEN:

Alexander, Brian. "Myth, Busted: You Only Use 10 Percent of Brain." *NBC News*, April 18, 2012. https://www.nbcnews.com/healthmain/myth-busted-you-only-use-10-percent-brain-1c9386687.

Brandon Lucero.com. "The New Generation Entrepreneur." Accessed December 6, 2021. https://brandonlucero.com/.

Carver, Leo, and Melissa Carver. "5 Ways to Develop Your Intuition." Chopra.com, January 25, 2016. https://chopra.com/articles/5-ways-develop-your-intuition.

Maidique, Modesto A. "Intuition Isn't Just About Trusting your Gut." *Harvard Business Review*, April 13, 2011. https://hbr.org/2011/04/intuition-good-bad-or-indiffer.

Peak Wellbeing. "The Reason for Repetition: How Repetition Helps Us Learn." Peak Wellbeing, February 3, 2016. https://medium.com/peak-wellbeing/the-reason-for-repetition-how-repetition-helps-us-learn-10d7eea43e95.

Puiu, Tibi. "Going with Your Gut: Decision-Making Based on Instinct Alone 90% Accurate of the Time, Study Shows." ZME Science, August 10, 2018. https://www.zmescience.com/research/studies/decision-making-intuition-accurate-42433/.

Resnick, Brian. "'Reality' Is Constructed by Your Brain: Here's What That Means, and Why It Matters." *Vox*, June 22, 2020. https://www.vox.com/science-and-health/20978285/optical-illusion-science-humility-reality-polarization.

Riggio, Ronald E. "Women's Intuition: Myth or Reality? It's Mostly Reality." *Psychology Today* (blog), July 14, 2011. https://www.psychologytoday.com/us/blog/cutting-edge-leadership/201107/women-s-intuition-myth-or-reality.

Tabaka, Marla. "Iconic Entrepreneurs Use Their Intuition to Succeed." *Inc.*, September 30, 2019. https://www.inc.com/marla-tabaka/iconic-entrepreneurs-use-their-intuition-to-succeed-what-you-need-to-know-about-following-your-gut.html.

Wilding, Melody. "The Science of Intuition Can Help You Understand How to Use It." *Quartz*, March 14, 2018. https://qz.com/work/1227997/the-science-of-intuition-can-help-you-understand-how-to-use-it/.

Chapter Eight:

Cain, Áine. "5 Years after Facebook Exec Sheryl Sandberg's Famous Book Told Women to 'Lean In,' It Appears That Advice May Have Mixed Results." *Insider*, August 6, 2018. https://www.businessinsider.co.za/facebook-sheryl-sandberg-lean-in-problematic-advice-2018-8.

Chkhetia, Shalva. "Repetition Is Key." LinkedIn, October 20, 2019. https://www.linkedin.com/pulse/repetition-mother-learning-father-action-which-makes-zig-chkhetia/.

Cohen, Ilene Strauss. "How to Let Go of the Need to Be Perfect." *Psychology Today* (blog), January 12, 2018. https://www.psychologytoday.com/us/blog/your-emotional-meter/201801/how-let-go-the-need-be-perfect.

DeCesare, Hilary, and Jim Fortin. "Episode 9: You Are Never Stuck." Produced by The ReLaunch Co. *The Silver Lined* ReLaunch. October 6, 2021. Podcast, MP3 audio, 6:56. https://therelaunchco.com/podcast-episode-9-you-are-never-stuck/.

Emaus, Todd. "Why Work Life Alignment, Not Balance, Is the Key to Happiness." *Forbes*, June 13, 2017. https://www.forbes.com/sites/theyec/2017/06/13/why-work-life-alignment-not-balance-is-the-key-to-happiness/? sh=6afb8bfb7bac.

Faure, Charles, Annabelle Limballe, and Hugo A. Kerhervé. "Fooling the Brain, Fooling the Pain: The Role of Mirror Therapy and Modern Uses in Virtual Reality." *Frontiers for Young Minds*, July 3, 2019. https://kids.frontiersin.org/articles/10.3389/frym.2019.00091.

Goodreads. "Nora Ephron: Quotes; Quotable Quote." Accessed December 6, 2021. https://www.goodreads.com/quotes/906475-in-these-days-of-physical-fitness-hair-dye-and-plastic.

Jackson, Eric. "Sun Tzu's 31 Best Pieces of Leadership Advice." *Forbes*, May 23, 2014. https://www.forbes.com/sites/ericjackson/2014/05/23/sun-tzus-33-best-pieces-of-leadership-advice/?sh=64a69abf5e5e.

Kolbert, Elizabeth. "Why Facts Don't Change Our Minds." *New Yorker*, February 19, 2017. https://www.newyorker.com/magazine/2017/02/27/why-facts-dont-change-our-minds.

Longman, Molly. "This Is How Long It Really Takes to Form a Habit (Hint: It's Not 21 Days)." *Refinery29*, January 13, 2020. https://www.refinery29.com/en-us/2020/01/9183127/21-day-rule-form-a-habit-in-21-days.

Morgan, Blake. "Turn Your Day around with One Simple Habit from Mel Robbins." *Forbes*, October 11, 2021. https://www.forbes.com/sites/blakemorgan/2021/10/11/turn-your-day-around-with-one-simple-habit-from-mel-robbins/?sh-=6b44870d3727.

MelRobbins.com. "Homepage." Accessed December 8, 2021. https://melrobbins.com/.

News18. "Humans Have Around 6,200 Thoughts in a Single Day, Shows New Study." July 19, 2020. https://www.news18.com/news/buzz/humans-have-around-6200-thoughts-in-a-single-day-shows-new-study-2723281.html.

Riggio, Ronald E. "5 Ways to Re-Align Your Life." *Psychology Today* (blog), December 13, 2019. https://www.psychologytoday.com/us/blog/cutting-edge-leadership/201912/5-ways-re-align-your-life.

Robins, Mel, and Rich Roll. "Confidence is a Habit & Motivation is Crap." *The Rich Roll Podcast*. October 29, 2020. Podcast, MP3 audio, 2:14:57. https://www.richroll.com/podcast/mel-robbins-630/.

CHAPTER NINE:

Becker, Emily. "35 Best Vision Board Quotes to Inspire You to Go After Your Goals in 2022." *Women's Health*, March 8, 2021. https://www.womenshealthmag.com/life/a35354813/vision-board-quotes/.

Buzzell, Amelia. "How to Manifest Love into Your Life Using the Law of Attraction, According to an Expert." PureWow, February 9, 2021. https://www.purewow.com/wellness/how-to-manifest-love.

Davis, Tchiki. "What Is Manifestation? Science-Based Ways to Manifest." *Psychology Today* (blog), September 15, 2020. https://www.psychologytoday.com/us/blog/click-here-happiness/202009/what-is-manifestation-science-based-ways-manifest.

Goldsmith, Barton. "The Art and Practice of Visualization." *Psychology Today* (blog), February 15, 2013. https://www.psychologytoday.com/us/blog/emotional-fitness/201302/the-art-and-practice-visualization.

Morin, Amy. "Why Vision Boards Don't Work (And What You Should Do Instead)." *Inc.*, November 16, 2018. https://www.inc.com/amy-morin/science-says-your-vision-board-actually-decreases-chances-of-living-your-dreams-heres-what-to-do-instead.html.

New Paradigm Advisors. "The BE-DO-HAVE Principle." January 27, 2021. https://newparadigmadvisors.com/the-be-do-have-principle/#:~:-text=Zig%20Ziglar%20regularly%20taught%20the,in%20life%20that%20really%20matter.

Park, Denise C., and Chih-Mao Huang. "Culture Wires the Brain: A Cognitive Neuroscience Perspective." *Perspectives on Psychological Science* 5, no. 4 (July 2010): 391–400. https://www.ncbi.nlm.nih.gov/pmc/articles/PMC3409833/.

Wong, Kenneth. "How to Use the Law of Vibration to Manifest." The Millennial Grind (blog), May 10, 2021. https://millennial-grind.com/how-to-use-the-law-of-vibration-to-manifest/.

CHAPTER TEN:

Kunst, Jennifer. "Let the Small Steps Count." *Psychology Today* (blog), November 9, 2011. https://www.psychologytoday.com/us/blog/headshrink-ers-guide-the-galaxy/201111/let-the-small-steps-count.

CHAPTER ELEVEN:

Barrett, Lisa Feldman. *How Emotions Are Made: The Secret Life of the Brain*. Boston: Mariner, 2017.

Baumgartner, Natalie. "Build a Culture That Aligns with People's Values." *Harvard Business Review*, April 8, 2020. https://hbr.org/2020/04/build-a-culture-that-aligns-with-peoples-values.

Cal Poly San Luis Obispo. "Learn by Doing." Accessed October 30, 2021. https://academicprograms.calpoly.edu/content/academicpolicies/learn-by-doing.

Cannon, Bradley. "All about Gratefulness with Robert A. Emmons, PhD." *Psi Chi* 21, no. 4 (Summer 2017). https://doi.org/10.24839/1092-0803.eye21.4.10.

Create Something Out of Nothing. "Oprah Winfrey Creating a Media Empire out of Nothing." Medium, October 17, 2018. https://medium.com/@createsomethingoutofnothing/how-o-prah-winfrey-created-a-media-empire-out-of-nothing-c4d4d20cbbfa.

DeCesare, Hilary, and Kara Goldin. "Episode 53: How to Overcome Doubts and Follow the 'Hints.'" Produced by The ReLaunch Co. *The Silver Lined* ReLaunch. April 14, 2021. Podcast, MP3 audio, 46:09. https://therelaunchco.com/podcast- episode-53-how-to-overcome-doubts-and-follow-the-hints-with-kara-goldin/.

Downes, Sophie. "How Hint Water's Kara Goldin Went from Zero Industry Experience to a $150 Million Business Empire." *Inc.*, November 10, 2020. https://www.inc.com/sophie-downes/hint-water-kara-goldin-en-trepreneur-advice-undaunted.html.

Duke, Annie. "Why Your Brain Clings to False Beliefs (Even When It Knows Better)." *Fast Company*, February 11, 2018. https://www.fastcompany.com/40528587/why-your-brain-clings-to-false-beliefs-even-when-it-knows-better.

Encyclopedia.com. "Oprah Evolves." Accessed November 21, 2021. https://www.encyclopedia.com/women/culture-magazines/oprah-evolves.

Folgers. "Pants: 15; Coffee Commercial; Folgers." YouTube Video, January 28, 2021. https://www.youtube.com/watch?v=UyR7lf- QpFo(Post Removed).

Fortune Editors. "How CEO Kara Goldin Kept Doubters from Crushing Her Vision for Hint Water." *Fortune*, March 31, 2021. https://fortune.com/2021/03/31/hint-water-ceo-kara-goldin/.

Glaser, Judith E. "The Neuroscience of Identity." *Psychology Today* (blog), July 17, 2019. https://www.psychologytoday.com/us/blog/conversational-intelligence/201907/the-neuroscience-identity.

Jean-Georges. "ABCV." Accessed November 22, 2021. https://http://www.huffpost.com/entry/85-of-what-we-worry-about_b_8028368 york/abcv.

Johnson, Megan. "Oprah Winfrey Discusses Teen Suicide Thoughts." *Boston Herald*, January 19, 2011. https://www.bostonherald.com/2011/01/19/oprah-winfrey-discusses-teen-suicide-thoughts/.

Mindspo. "Tip #6: Go Within and Connect." August 12, 2020. https://mindspo.com/2020/08/12/oprahs-top-10-rules-for-self-love/#:~:text=Go%20within%20and%20connect,that%20all%20things%20are%20possible.%E2%80%9D.

Peak Wellbeing. "The Reason for Repetition: How Repetition Helps Us Learn." February 3, 2016. https://medium.com/peak- wellbeing/the-reason-for-repetition-how-repetition-helps-us-learn-10d7eea43e95.

PwC. "PwC Pulse Survey: Next in Work." Accessed October 20, 2021. http://www.huffpost.com/entry/85-of-what-we-worry-about_b_8028368 survey/future-of-work.html.

ScienceDirect. "Self and Identity." Accessed December 3, 2021. https://www.sciencedirect.com/topics/social-sciences/self-and-identity.

Smith, Jeremy Adam. "How to Find Your Purpose in Life." *Greater Good Magazine*, January 10, 2018. https://greatergood.berkeley.edu/article/item/how_to_find_your_purpose_in_life.

Starseed Kitchen. "What Are High Vibration Foods." June 6, 2020. https://starseedkitchen.com/what-are-high-vibration-foods/.

Winfrey, Oprah. "Oprah's Letter to Her Younger Self." Oprah.com. Accessed December 9, 2021. https://www.oprah.com/spirit/oprahs-letter-to-her-younger-self-oprah-wisdom.

CHAPTER TWELVE:

Activities, Recreation, & Care for Individuals with Developmental Disabilities. "About." Greatergood.com, accessed November 19, 2021. https://greatergood.berkeley.edu/article/item/how_gratitude_changes_you_and_your_brain.

Business Wire. "Blackstone Buys Majority Stake in SPANX, Inc." October 20, 2021. https://www.businesswire.com/news/home/20211020005757/en/Blackstone-Buys-Majority-Stake-in-SPANX-Inc.

Bigman, Dan, and Dale Buss. "The Remarkable Power of Gratitude." *Chief Executive*, July 19, 2021. https://chiefexecutive.net/the-remarkable-power-of-gratitude/.

Blakely, Sara. "Behind the Scenes." Instagram, October 21, 2021. https://www.instagram.com/p/CVT1zswDZIL/?hl=en. Borysenko, Karlyn. "Real Examples of How Leaders Show Gratitude to Their Team." *Forbes*, November 26, 2019. https://www.forbes.com/sites/karlynborysenko/2019/11/26/real-examples-of-how-leaders-show-gratitude-to-their-team/?sh-=7e92ef5f72f5.

Brower, Tracy. "Gratitude Is a Key to Happiness: 4 Reasons Why." *Forbes*, April 25, 2021. https://www.forbes.com/sites/tracybrower/2021/04/25/gratitude-is-a-key-to-happiness-4-reasons-why/? sh=63bb9a69347c.

Brown, Joshua, and Joel Wong. "How Gratitude Changes You and Your Brain." *Greater Good Magazine*, June 6, 2017. https://greatergood.berkeley.edu/article/item/how_gratitude_changes_you_and_your_brain.

Chowdhury, Madhuleena Roy. "The Neuroscience of Gratitude and How It Affects Anxiety & Grief." PositivePsychology, July 1, 2022. https://positivepsychology.com/neuroscience-of-gratitude/.

Cornell University Graduate School Alumni Newsletter. "The Gratitude Project." Winter 2018. https://gradschool.cornell.edu/alumni/alumni-newsletter/the-gratitude-project/.

DeCesare, Hilary, and Alexsys Thompson. "Episode 56: How Gratitude Can Amplify Your Life and Leadership." Produced by The ReLaunch Co. *The Silver Lined* ReLaunch. May 5, 2021. Podcast, MP3 audio, 36:42.

https://therelaunchco.com/podcast-episode-56-how-gratitude-can-amplify-your-life-and-leadership-with-alexsys- thompson/.

Elton, Chester. *Leading with Gratitude*. New York: Harper Business, 2020.

Emmons, Robert. "How Gratitude Can Help You Through Hard Times." *Greater Good Magazine*, May 13, 2013. https://greatergood.berkeley.edu/article/item/how_gratitude_can_help_you_through_hard_times.

Frontiers. "The Neurobiology of Gratitude." Accessed November 12, 2021. https:// www.frontiersin.org/research- topics/18327/the-neurobiology-of-gratitude.

Harvard Health Publishing. "Giving Thanks Can Make You Happier." August 14, 2021. https://www.health.harvard.edu/healthbeat/giving-thanks-can-make-you-happier.

Mosley, Eric. "The Business Impact of Gratitude." *Forbes*, November 27, 2019. https://www.forbes.com/sites/ericmosley/2019/11/27/the-business-impact-of-gratitude/?sh=7e95e86d630c.

Neurohealth Associates. "Neuroscience Reveals: Gratitude Literally Rewires Your Brain to be Happier." Neurohealth, July 4, 2020. https://nhahealth.com/neuroscience-reveals-gratitude-literally-rewires-your-brain-to-be-happier/.

Spanx. "About Us." Accessed October 31, 2021. https://SPANX.com/pages/about-us.

Spanx. "Making the World a Better Place ... Together." Accessed October 30, 2021. https://spanx.com/pages/elevatingwomen.

Chapter Thirteen:

American Psychological Association. "Building Your Resilience." January 1, 2012, updated February 1, 2020. https://www.apa.org/topics/resilience.

DeCesare, Hilary, and Cali Gilbert. "Episode 83: How to Manifest Your Dream Life by Trusting Your Intuition." Produced by The ReLaunch Co. *The Silver Lined* ReLaunch. November 10, 2021. Podcast, MP3 audio, 25:12. https://therelaunchco.com/podcast-episode-83-how-to-manifest-your-dream-life-by-trusting-your-intuition-with-cali- gilbert/.

Goodreads. "Books by Cali Gilbert." Accessed December 20, 2021. https://www.goodreads.com/author/list/6031570.Cali_Gilbert.

Lebsack, Lexy. "Can Beauty Change the Face of Homelessness?" *Refinery29*, May 11, 2019. https://www.refinery29.com/en-ca/2019/05/232582/homeless-women-hair-beauty-services-los-angeles.

Tower 15 Productions. "F.E.M.A.L.E Alliance." Accessed November 15, 2021. https://www.tower15productions.com/femalealliance.html.

CHAPTER FOURTEEN:

DeCesare, Hilary, and Erica Miller. "Episode 74: How to Live a Long Life and Live it Well with Dr. Erica Miller." Produced by The ReLaunch Co. *The Silver Lined* ReLaunch. September 8, 2021. Podcast, MP3 audio, 41:21. https://therelaunchco.com/podcast-episode-74-how-to-live-a-long-life-and-live-it-well-with-dr-erica-miller/.

Wong, Y., Jesse Owen, Nicole Gabana, Joshua Brown, Sydney McInnis, Paul Toth, and Lynn Gilman. "Does Gratitude Writing Improve the Mental Health of Psychotherapy Clients? Evidence from a Randomized Controlled Trial." *Psychotherapy Research* 28, no. 2 (2018): 192–202. https://pubmed.ncbi.nlm.nih.gov/27139595/.

Young, Myrna. "How to Apply, the Law of Divine Oneness, to Your Life." Transform You Mind (blog), December 8, 2020. https://blog.myhelps.us/how-apply-law-divine-oneness-to-life/.

POSTSCRIPT

Davidson, Paul. "'I Let Money Get in the Way': Most Recent Job Quitters Have Regrets or Don't Plan to Stay in New Role." USA Today, March 28, 2022. https://www.usatoday.com/story/money/2022/03/28/great-resignation-regret-workers-quit-jobs-not-content/7163041001/?gnt-cfr=1.

Stillman, Jessica. "The Great Resignation Is Turning into the Great Regret." Inc., n.d., accessed August 16, 2022. https://www.inc.com/jessica-stillman/hiring-great-resignation-great-regret.html.